THE LAST MASS
OF PAUL VI

An autumn night's dream

The Last Mass of Paul VI

An Autumn Night's Dream

TITO CASINI

Angelico Press

CATHOLIC TRADITIONALIST CLASSICS

This Angelico Press edition is a reprint
of the work originally published in 1971
by Britons Publishing Company.
Angelico Press, 2024

For information, address:
Angelico Press, Ltd.
169 Monitor St.
Brooklyn, NY 11222
www.angelicopress.com

Paperback: 979-8-88677-096-4
Hardcover: 979-8-88677-097-1

Cover design
by Michael Schrauzer

TABLE OF CONTENTS

TRANSLATOR'S NOTE

This is a poor translation done by an amateur working against time. None the less, such is the excellence of the original that it will certainly still shine through.

Tito Casini could well in our day be that Timothy to whom the Apostle Paul wrote: Praedica verbum, insta opportune, importune; argue, obsecra, increpa in omni patientia et doctrina. Erit enim tempus cum sanam doctrinam, non sustinebunt sed ad sua desideria coacervabunt, magistros, prurientes auribus, et a veritate quidem auditum avertent, ad fabulas autem convertentur. Tu vero vigila, in omnibus labora, opus fac evangelistae, ministerium tuum imple. - *As Italy's best-known Catholic writer, he has done just that.*

I should like to inscribe on his book what has been carved upon the tomb of my illustrious countryman, that other devout and learned exponent of Catholic doctrine in the full Latin tradition, John Duns Scotus:

DECUIT - POTUIT - FECIT.

He has indeed carried out what he was well fitted to do, and what he knew to be right. He has become the authentic voice of the "Church of All Ages". With the help of God, his efforts will not have been in vain.

Scott McCallum

For the Church of all Ages

"I have a dream...". In these words, borrowed from Luther King, Cardinal Suenens, primate of Belgium, not excluded by reason of age from electing or being elected to the Papacy, expressed last September his active hopes for a "Future World Church", with a new Creed and relevant restructurisation, towards which the Church of today, with its reform and cult of reform, would represent the stage of transition.

Loyal to the Church of all ages, the Holy Church of God into which I was born, within which I strive, in which I intend to die, and in the not inactive conviction of a return from present-day aberrations to the path of her true *Credo*, of her fervent *Adoro*, I too have had a dream which, in these latest pages of mine, I would recount to my friends.

"Autumn Night's Dream" it might be called, for it happened around November 30th; and in all its first part it was like a nightmare on awakening from which one says, with that pleasure which is child of pain "Oh, thank God it's not true!"; whilst the second part would draw forth the cry: "Oh, if only it were!".

A dream, in any case, it was, fortunately for its ugliness and unhappily for its beauty, fruit of a love identical both for the Church and for him who, with sometimes trembling and uncertain hand, wields those keys of hers which he himself has called heavy; a love,

7

a burning love — like that described in the Canticle: *"fortis est ut mors dilectio"* (love strong as death) — that has inspired all those other books of mine, of which this forms the natural sequel and may well conclude the cycle.

Natural it is, coming after *La Tunica Stracciata* (The Torn Tunic) in which I began my battle; after *Dicebamus Heri* (As We Said Yesterday), where I replied to the resultant counter-attacks; after *Super Flumina Babylonis* (By the Waters of Babylon), the exile of defeat; after *Ricorso a Maria* (Recourse to Mary), the appeal — that appeal which I know will be answered, but which I fain would see answered through action of Paul VI; and so, then, to my dream.

Qui habet somnium, says Jeremiah, *narret somnium*, (He who has a dream, let him tell his dream). It is precisely what I have done. And may Mary indulging my human impatience quickly bring the beauty of that dream to pass, persuading Jesus, as she did at Cana, to hasten for us His hour.

To this end, that the wine of faith may never fail, I too shall give my utmost effort, not dreaming merely but doing, as Mary would want: *"Quodcumque dixerit vobis facite"* (Do whatever He should tell you); as He would want: *"Implete hydrias..."* (Fill up the water-jars). And no other end, no other pretension, does this book possess than that of one small offering, a little water from the lowliest of Christ's servants, that He may indeed perform the miracle and that, His glory being again made manifest, all may believe, or turn once more to their belief, in Him.

Florence, *in Conceptione Immaculata Beatae Mariae Virginis, 1970.*

TITO CASINI

8

Departure with the Angelus

In his dark travelling-suit, looking out through the window of his plane as it prepared for take-off, Paul VI ("Montini" for the new-style Catholics who seldom or never used Holiness or Holy Father) raised his arms in that habitual gesture of his to take leave of the group of dignitaries gathered in his honour at Fiumicino. His gaze then travelled on beyond them towards Rome. Through breaks in a curtain of gold and purple cloud, the rising sun lit up and threw into strong relief the major basilicas of St. Peter's and St. Paul's; and from the heart of the Pope there welled up to his lips the hymn that had been recited for centuries in the first Vespers of the two Apostles:

> 'O Roma felix quae duorum Principum
> Es consacrata glorioso sanguine!
> Horum cruore purpurata caeteras
> Excellis orbis una pulchritudine!'

(O happy Rome, who in thy martyr princes' blood,
A twofold stream, art washed and doubly sanctified!
All earthly beauty thou alone outshinest far, empurpled by their out poured life-blood's glorious tide!)

Thus, in Latin, did the words come to him — from force of habit, despite the new law to which he too had assented, that recital of the Office be purely vol-

9

untary, even if recommended, not imposed as a duty or "*officium*", and anyhow in the vernacular. At the same moment, remembering whose the verses were, there sprang again to his mind that other Latin which he had tried so unsuccessfully to forget; Latin wherein the two Apostles once again appeared; whose ever-recurrent recollection was a torture to him. It sounded just like one of the old oracular prophecies; but for him, ever since that far-off 3rd of April 1969, its meaning had been all too clear! "*Si quis autem hoc attentare praesumpserit, indignationem omnipotentis Dei, ac beatorum Petri et Pauli Apostolorum eius, se noverit incursurum*". (If anyone should dare to alter this, let him know that he incurs the wrath of Almighty God, and of His blessed Apostles Peter and Paul) — After that 3rd of April 1969 those words of warning and of menace were aimed directly at him, the man who had dared; and Paul VI, yet once more, shuddered.

From an ancient church nearby, rung perhaps by some aged priest faithful to custom, as some still were, a bell pealed out on the morning air. The new churches generally had no steeple, no finger pointed towards heaven, for sirens had substituted the consecrated bells, being considered more modern, more in keeping with the worker spirit which now laid claim, before God, to that "fruit of our labour" duly inserted in the Mass.

The Pope, drawing back from the window and making the sign of the Cross, devoutly began to say the *Angelus*. Devoutly, as always, but now more than ever, perturbed as he was again by those words.

"*Angelus Domini nuntiavit Mariae, et concepit de Spiritu Sancto. Ave Maria, gratia plena...*"

He had great love for Our Lady, and in her he placed his trust. Conscious of his human frailty, of his frailty as Peter through the weakness of Simon, he invoked her assistance, to strengthen him and to lift him up in every crisis and after every failure; and among his most frequent, deeply-felt prayers, said sometimes with tears but half-hidden, was the one he used to say as a seminarist in the Little Office of Our Lady: *"Concede, misericors Deus, fragilitati nostrae praesidium..."*. (Grant, O merciful God, in defence of our frailty...).

That frailty of his! He had confessed to it in a sad speech, again during the same long-gone, ever-present 1969; he had recognised himself to be "only a man", likening himself to that other man who by reason of his human frailty had received from Christ the heaviest of censures: "Get thee behind me, Satan. Thou art an obstacle in my path!" — barely an hour after his faith had been rewarded by the supreme praise: "Thou art a happy man. Because it is not flesh and blood that revealed this to thee but my Father in heaven". In tones of one accusing rather than defending himself, he had said on that 10th of September in St. Peter's: *"Homo sum"* (I am but a man). And then: "Peter also, or rather Simon, was weak and inconstant, alternating attitudes of enthusiasm with those of fear"; and he ended with, "we must throw ourselves at the feet of Christ, repeating to Him with infinite humility Peter's own words: *Homo peccator sum* (I am a sinful man); but adding also with immense love: *Tu scis quia amo Te* (Thou knowest that I love Thee)".

The roar of the engines full open for departure had drowned the last peals of the bell when one of his party, wearing a grey suit with a pullover underneath the jacket, appeared and stopped — with respectful confidence — at the door of the Pope's small compartment, just as he had finished his *Angelus*. He was at

11

once asked to come in: "Come in, Cardinal, and sit down!" Then, smiling and pointing to the seat next to his own, he added: "You have caught me in the act; still praying in Latin; but I do hope you will forgive me, for, what with that sky, that view of Rome."

Cardinal Bugnini, with his plump, complacent face, smiled in turn:

"Indeed, indeed! I too, truth to tell, sometimes... certain habits die hard... But not so with our new priests, brought up as they are on Cardinal Garrone's *Ratio Fundamentalis!*" Here he passed witty comment on that article of the regulations governing seminary studies which, in place of the solid grasp of former times, had substituted "*a suitable knowledge* of the Latin tongue". This, according to him, meant a moderate ability to decline *rosa-rosae*.

Cardinal Bugnini, Prefect — or as he preferred, Minister of the Congregation — or "Ministry" — for Divine Worship, had just recently persuaded the Pope to abandon the final small remnant of Latin prayer to which he had seemed to cling as to the last vestige of the Church's language. — ("*Lingua Ecclesiae et cum Ecclesiae vita perpetuo coniuncta*" his predecessor Pope John had described it[1].) (Language of the Church, bound up forever with the Church's life.) — It was the Latin *Angelus* recited by him at noon every Sunday from the famous window along with the mass of Romans and foreigners gathered in the Square below. He had presuaded or induced him to give way, painful though it had been, by reminding him with discreet insistence of the promise contained in his speech, from that same window, on the date to which the liturgical revolution traced its rise, March 7th 1965. It was a rise, as cautious as the situation demanded, towards the global aim which he had in mind; for which he used Paul VI like some Louis XVI, to be led from concession to concession, from one surrender to the next, right up to the woollen cap and the guillotine.

"This Sunday", the Pope had then said[2] "marks a memorable date in the spiritual history of the Church, because the spoken language makes its official entry into the Church's liturgy... to make her prayers intelligible and have them understood". Ill-concealing a reluctance springing possibly from foreboding of other memorable dates along the road to that rationalisation of religion which would end little short of a religion of rationalisation, he had added: "It is a sacrifice which the Church has effected of her own language, Latin: a language that is sacred, grave, beautiful, extremely impressive and elegant. She has sacrificed the traditions of centuries; and above all she sacrifices a unity of language between the various peoples, in homage to this greater universality of reaching all men". But, immediately and logically contradicting himself, at sight of the faithful down there below, of the "various peoples" with whom he could not pray in any "unity of language" save in their "own language" as Catholics, he recited the *Angelus* in Latin, after introducing it thus: "We shall still pray to Our Lady, for the present, in Latin..." *Still, for the present.* The irresolution, the constitutional hamletic make-up of Paul VI revealed itself in these two adverbial expressions, which, so much at variance, expressed his will to resist, to *guard the deposit*, and at the same time his disposition to yield to the "innovators" who were firmly bent on destroying everything, from the beginnings of form, language and rite to the conclusions of substance, dogma and faith.

In these their separate and opposed views and intents, that *Angelus*, that brief prayer "still" said in

Latin, had thus a great symbolic value for the Pope and for Cardinal Bugnini who, leader of the innovators, had now with his elevation to the purple and investiture as head of the Prefecture for Divine Worship reached the apex of his liturgical career.

It had not been easy for the Cardinal to bring the Pope to this surrender. He had succeeded by insisting on that "for the present" which obviously could not mean "forever" and had to imply a time-limit. The fact of foreigners being always present in the square of St. Peter's, often in greater numbers than the Romans, should not make the Pope forget, he said, that he was Bishop of Rome, a Bishop praying with the faithful of his diocese in their own language...; and when the Pope asked him with a smile whether he should say the *Angelus* in *romanesco*, or Roman dialect, he had replied unsmilingly: "And why not? Dialects, you know..."

And indeed dialects were now playing an increasingly large part in the "reformed liturgy"; it was calculated that there were by now thousands of "Masses", or kinds of "Mass", or "agapes", or "suppers"; versions of the Mass, that is to say, or rather imitations (where they were not parodies) so different from it and so discordant that, in the greater part of them, it would have been hard to recognise the original or essential content. It was enough to leave one's own "Diocesan Community" to find oneself, in church, among strangers.

Still unconvinced of the validity of the argument, the Pope had continued to defend his *Angelus* by recalling that in Uganda he had *had* to celebrate Mass in Latin, at the request of the local population, and that in Bogotà and at Fatima the voices surrounding him had joyfully swelled forth each time he had turned from the Spanish or Portuguese vernacular to the Latin used for the *Gloria*, the *Credo* or the *Agnus Dei*. He had defended his *Angelus* and his Latin even in the name of poetry, quoting those verses of Moretti's *Ultima Estate* (The Last Summer) which he liked so much:

"Il Pontefice appare alla finestra
da cui pende l'arazzo con le chiavi

* * *

Indugia il Santo Padre alla finestra

* * *

Benedictio Dei omnipotentis,
Patris et Filii et Spiritus Sancti,
Descendat super vos et maneat semper".

(The Pontiff appears at the window whence hang the tapestried keys. The Holy Father at the window lingers. May the blessing of Almighty God, Father, Son and Holy Ghost, descend upon you and remain with you forever.)

But what was poetry or beauty itself for these Jacobins of the Reform? And Cardinal Bugnini, their head, had ended by wresting this too from "his king"; the Pope now said his public *Angelus* in Italian; an Angelus re-written by the translators, in full accord with the modern exegesists of Sacred Scripture, which is to say taking into account their "demythologising" of this same, in great part now considered to be just exactly that, a work of poetry.

The Annunciation as represented by Luke, the painter evangelist, had found the experts of the "Oecumenical Commission" entrusted with production of the new common Bible (Catholics, Protestants, Jews, Mos-

15

lems, and Free-thinkers), all in complete agreement. It was held to be an "invention", and so the "Angel" no longer figured in the new text, just as "conceived by the Holy Ghost" was also omitted, whilst Our Lady was expressly and markedly referred to as "wife of Joseph the carpenter".

The worker complex now in fashion had inspired the "prayer" invoking her as "Mother of the Workers", and, in confiding their cause to her patronage, had expressed the hope that she would be "harbinger of a new era of peace in social justice". Unhappy in its form, like all substitutions for the Latin, the new text had, however, as well as its oecumenism, one advantage over the other in the eyes of the Pope: it "explicitised", as had been explained to him, "the sociology implicit in the message of Nazareth", and that had led him to accept its form with a lesser "sacrifice" than would otherwise have been the case.

The cause of the workers, peace in social justice, oecumenism, these were vibrant chords in the heart of Paul VI, — hamletic, yes, but leaning to the left; and it was for this that he now found himself aboard the plane about to take off on the most "daring" yet of the Pope's many journeys. The destination and symbols, the members of his party, all told just how much distance the Church had covered in this direction: the Church represented by him who did not always represent himself, torn as he was even now between the throb of the engines at departure and that solitary bell to whose pealing he had "still" said his *Angelus*.

For Peace in Justice

He did love Our Lady, not with a hamletic but a steadfast love, and as in all his travels, he had desired her image to accompany him on the aeroplane now carrying him so far away from Rome.

It was a *Ma-Ma*, a very powerful, very modern four-engined jet, deriving its title from the initial syllables of Mao and Marx; and when he had accepted the aged President's invitation, it had been sent to bring him to Peking. The negotiations for the encounter between the Catholic Church and this most extreme form of Communism (extreme also in its war upon the "opium of religion") had been difficult and protracted; and it was only right that among guests of honour should be Cardinal Casaroli who also, for his skill in bringing them to a successful conclusion, had earned for himself what was still improperly called "the purple". (Improperly, since this noble and meaningful garb had fallen into disuse. Those elevated by Paul VI were all imbued with the concepts of "anti-triumphalism", "democracy", and "the church of the poor", even though not disdaining the privileges which the rank conferred.)

Run as it now was by elements all "open to the left", the Vatican had not offered any objection based on principle to the negotiations, to the "direct dialogue"

17

with Communism. Indeed Paul VI in person, consumed by his intense desire for peace in social justice, had several times taken the initiative, disregarding questions of protocol which were meant to preserve his dignity, and refusing to be discouraged by repeated rebuffs.

Everyone remembered his personal approaches, all of them failures, to the heads of the Communist governments most bitterly hostile to the Holy See and to the Church. The memory was still fresh of the *cigarettes* he offered to Podgorny, President of the Soviet Union, who on his return to Russia had repaid the compliment by intensifying attacks upon religion and in particular upon that Catholicism which Lenin had rightly considered "the only real obstacle to the triumph of Communism". It had been made known to Ochab, the Polish President who had insolently refused him entry to his country, that on the occasion of his visit to the Quirinal he would be more than happy to receive him with full honours in the Vatican. And the casual contempt with which his "cigarettes", so to speak, were refused did nothing to damp his ardour and optimism, bent as he was — or at any rate as his advisers were — on offering the hand of friendship to Communism, and on gripping any hand offered in return, even if, through the errors of men, it turned out at times to be a clenched fist, and indeed a bloodstained one.

The delay with which, despite his desire, this meeting had been arranged was not due to any hesitation on his part as to its suitability, but to the conflict between the two Communist currents in the Vatican, about which he was perplexed and uncertain; the

"Russian" one logically wished him to go to Moscow, whilst the "Chinese" one wanted him in Peking.

Moscow could be said, in a certain sense, to have merited priority, because it was there that the shuttle-work had originally begun. The journey had commenced, in secret, from there, though it was ending up today at Peking. Communism in those days had had only one soul; and in this too, for the end sought, there had been concerted action. Already in control of the official Russian Church, it exploited that situation to get itself into position against its principal foe, the Catholic Church; and using the Metropolitan Nicodemus, its spy and able secret agent, it had succeeded through the Archbishop of Paris, Cardinal Marty, in broaching the Vatican and making direct contact with Paul VI himself. Encouraged by Cardinal Willebrands, President of the Secretariate for the Union of Christians, and by Archbishop Casaroli. Secretary of the Congregation for Public Affairs, further approaches were subsequently made through the Metropolitan Filarete, ferocious government instrument in the destruction of the Catholic Church in the Ukraine, and persecutor of those Orthodox Christians still unwilling to conform. This, incidentally, was the man turned back at Rome, not by reason of any of the foregoing, but because of the well-founded opposition of the Italian police[3].

Not indeed by reason of the foregoing, for no sacrifice, no humiliation of the Church's children was too much for Paul VI in his strivings towards his "brethren", and no price outweighed the results he was hoping for from this "opening" of his. He himself invited them to calm down, to retire; and the purple was waiting in Rome for the various Berans and Slip-

19

ys who, unbent by all the years of imprisonment they had suffered for the faith in their own countries, now from obedience underwent the cruellest of their martyrdoms, that of self-exile, as had been arranged between the Vatican and their persecutors, so that others more acceptable might take their place.

Inflexible, despite all the efforts of Cardinal Koenig — who could well have adopted that well-known lament "Seven pairs of shoes have I worn out" — Mindszenty stayed on in Budapest. As the crestfallen Austrian primate himself confessed to a leading French newspaper[4]: "Reste la douloureuse affaire du Cardinal Mindszenty auquel je rends régulièrement visite. Nul n'ignore que le Saint Siège a proposé à l'auguste prélat de gagner Rome et d'y achever paisiblement ses jours. Quelque chose me dit que les autorités locales ne s'y seraient pas opposées; on aurait sans doute fermé les yeux. Mais le Cardinal Mindszenty a toujours refusé." However, what the blandishments of the Viennese Archbishop had not been able to accomplish was now achieved by death; and this voice too, the voice of his long silence, was no more. It had found its last expression in the words of his spiritual testament: "*Bonum certamen certavi, cursum consummavi, fidem servavi. In reliquo reposita est mihi corona iustitiae, quam reddet mihi Dominus in illa die iustus iudex.*" (I have fought the good fight, I have finished the race, I have kept the faith. For the rest there awaiteth me the crown of justice which the Lord, the just judge, will give unto me on that day).

Despite the government's orders to the contrary, all Hungary flocked to his funeral, so that there was fear of a repetition of 1956. The Pope's telegram and speech of condolence were sincere. But the "openers" remained undismayed; they were well accustomed to his hamletic qualities, and were equally aware of his basic propensity for counterbalancing each step backward with two longer ones forward. From the Catacombs of Domitilla it had gradually been possible to reach the present trip.

From the Catacombs of Domitilla

How much journeying there had been between there and here, what approaches to Communism — which had stayed exactly where it was. Stopping to celebrate Mass there on his way back from Castelgandolfo on September 12th 1965, he had said[5]: "By an all too easy association of ideas we are led to think here of those sectors of the Church which still today live in the catacombs... The very real analogies existing between the Church which still today is struggling, suffering, and barely surviving in those countries with atheistic and totalitarian regimes, and that of the ancient catacombs are evident. The motive inspiring the Church's resistance is the same today as it was then: to defend the Truth, and at the same time to uphold the sacred right of every man to his own individual freedom, especially in the basic area of conscience and religion. Identical too is the purpose of both ancient and modern persecutors who, by physical violence or by weight of legal, judicial, or administrative machinery seek to impose their own particular version of truth and to suffocate all contrary expressions of thought."

It is painful to see, he had added sadly, "how in so many countries which We yet highly esteem and love, after so much talk of freedom and of the people, it is now sought to stifle the religious life of that people and the individuals composing it; whilst towards the Church there exists the deliberate even if unspoken intention, the ungenerous desire, to suppress her: gradually it is made impossible to renew the ranks of the clergy, already heavily depleted; the normal exercise of pastoral government is obstructed when clergy, religious and faithful cannot be forced to collaborate with the regime; in order to filch youth from the Church and impose upon it the word of Marxism, all means at the disposal of totalitarian organisation are monopolised: — the vehicles of the press and of cultural, scholastic, educative and recreative life... You know these things... and it would be well for all Catholics... who by the grace of God live in freedom, to remember those other Catholics living in the modern catacombs; not to forget how sad, humanly speaking, is their fate, and to reflect that without vigilance and concord, a similar fate might well befall them too[5]."

Communism, both home and foreign, was logically not at all happy with this kind of talk from Paul VI. It was reminiscent of the stronger expressions of *Divini Redemptoris*, the most reasoned and resolute act of condemnation by which it had ever been denounced. Especially was it not happy at denunciation of its tactical camouflage, thus already unmasked and branded by Pius XI: "Communism at the outset showed what it was in all its perversity, but very soon it realised that in this way it was only alienating the peoples of the world, and it therefore changed tactics and now attempts to attract the masses by a variety of deceptions, camouflaging its real designs beneath ideas which in themselves are good and attractive. Thus, seeing a common desire for peace, the Communist leaders pretend to be the most zealous exponents and propagators of the movement for world peace; but at the same time they stir up a class war which produces rivers of blood; and feeling that they themselves have no internal guarantee of peace, they embark upon unlimited re-armament. Thus too, under various auspices totally unconnected with Communism, they form societies and found periodicals with the exclusive aim of infiltrating their ideas into spheres which otherwise would not be readily accessible to them; indeed they attempt in their cunning even to penetrate Catholic and religious associations. In the same way, elsewhere, without in the slightest degree abandoning their perverse principles, they invite Catholics to collaborate with them in the so-called humanitarian and charitable fields, going so far at times as to propose measures wholly in keeping with the Christian spirit and the doctrine of the Church. In yet other areas, they will push their hypocrisy so far as to make believe that Communism in countries of deeper faith and wider culture will take on a different, milder aspect, will not hinder the practice of religion, and will respect freedom of conscience. — Venerable Brothers, so act that the faithful be not deceived! Communism is intrinsically perverse, and in no field whatsoever can collaboration with it be envisaged by anyone desirous of preserving our Christian civilisation. And should there be people erroneously persuaded to co-operate in the victory of Communism in their various countries, it is they who will fall first victims to that error; and the more ancient and renowned the Christian civilisation of the regions which Communism succeeds in penetrating, the more destructive will the hatred of these enemies of God show itself to be."

Watchfulness... carefulness not to be deceived...; but that from which Paul today and Pius yesterday had warned the shepherds to save their sheep now had affected the shepherds themselves: whether as dupes or active connivers, the shepherds were hob-nobbing and flirting, as it were, with the wolves; with wolves to a greater or lesser extent dressed up in sheeps' clothing, and all of them bleating raucously about peace, co-existence, and collaboration in the cause of the poor... Rehabilitated now, and judged to be intrinsically sound, Communism had made its way into the Church. ("Ecclesiastical *Community*" it had begun to be called, diluting into an insipid adjective the glorious, solid substantive, and giving its ramifications similar treatment, as in "diocesan *Community*" instead of "diocese", and "parochial *Community*" instead of parish".) Communism existed also in the hierarchy, among its topmost representatives, even among those who surrounded the Shepherd of shepherds; and indeed it was here that it had its most solid defenders and its most active allies for the conquest of the flock.

This, on the tactical plane, had been its greatest victory; to this was due, in Italy, the red flag which flew this morning from the Quirinal and saluted the passage of the *Ma-Ma* carrying the Pope to the East; due to it also was the courtesy telegram which the exalted traveller had had despatched at once, and which began: "To the First People's Commissar of the Italian Socialist Republic. At the moment of setting out on Our journey of peace etc.".

It was due to it inasmuch as, during Vatican II, those aforesaid allies, the Communists inside the Church, had seen to it that no alarm was raised, no repetition permitted of the Domitilla speech, against what the Italian Bishop Carli of Segni defined "the greatest heresy of our times", what another, the

26

Chinese Yu Pin, called "the sum of all heresies", what yet another, the Russian Elko, termed "the plague of present-day society", and what the Slovak Hnilika described as "a species of pseudo-mystical body of Satan[5]."

On October 9th 1965 some five hundred Council Fathers from all parts of the world petitioned that the Council, as befitted such a solemn, extraordinary and universal assembly, should speak out condemning and warning against the doctrine and practice of something which, as Paul VI had so lately put it, harboured towards the Church "the deliberate even if unspoken intention, the ungenerous desire, to suppress her".

It was a proposal which could not fail to worry those who did indeed nurture this precise intention and left it unsaid only to make it more effective. It was essential that it fall through; and to achieve this the Communists turned to their agents in St. Peter's, who in fact served them so well that, in blatant disregard for the rules of the Council, the request was never even tabled or brought before the assembly. Pretexts were used which it would be ingenuous to call simply puerile, — like the one, for instance, which referred to the "pastoral nature" of the Council: as if, as was vainly pointed out, there was "any problem more pastoral than that of keeping the faithful from becoming atheists through Communism", of preventing the unsuspecting, defenceless sheep from finishing up as prey to the wolves.

The delight and appreciation of world Communism were proportionate to the value of the victory. Referring to it in the *Literaturnaja Gazeta*, Tass's Rome correspondent wrote[5]: "the organisers of this petition tried to frighten their Council colleagues; but their efforts were of no avail. The majority of the Bishops, for a variety of reasons, failed to support these obvious

27

reactionaries...". Moscow's representative, however, did not hide his disappointment at the fact that in one of the Council Schemes a note appeared which, in speaking of "atheistic doctrines" — though having the good taste not to mention Communism, the pulpit whence they were expounded — none the less did make reference to "documents of the four last Popes, among them the ferocious anti-Communist encyclicals of Pius XI and Pius XII"; but the hope, the accompanying implied request, that on these items too silence should be maintained by the Church was not to go unheard. Like all other interventions by the *Magisterium* in defence of our faith and of our civilisation against the evils and deceptions of Communism, the *Speech from the Catacombs* was to be considered taboo; and as for the most "ferocious" document, which is to say the most eloquent and fundamental of them, Pius XI's *Divini Redemptoris*, it is a fact that only one newspaper, sole exception among its principal colleagues, forgot its thirtieth anniversary in 1967, totally withholding any comment on it from its columns, and not even mentioning its name or its existence. This was the newspaper of the Holy See: the *Osservatore Romano*.

The Pilgrim of Reconciliation

The Chinese-Papal *Ma-Ma* was flying high and fast towards the East. Left far behind now, Rome was only barely discernible through the low cloud formations that spread across the Eternal City. Gazing towards it in a last farewell, the Pope nevertheless could see and recognise, from its dome emerging upon the Esquiline, the greatest of Our Lady's churches, Saint Mary Major's. He saw and recognised it, and he was happy to think of this as a favourable omen for his journey: happy that from there, which was like saying from her, there had come something like a response to his farewell.

Yes, he loved Our Lady, and no longer having to be careful about Cardinal Bugnini, who had gone, he murmured the first words of her feast *Sanctae Mariae ad Nives* (Our Lady of the Snows), now suppressed: *"Salve, sancta Parens..."* (Hail, holy Mother). But this was only a brief comfort, followed by another quiver of apprehension, similar to the one he had felt previously and due to the same sudden recollection. It was as though from his tomb there, in Saint Mary Major's, the words of his great and saintly predecessor had been spoken to him again: *"Si quis autem hoc attentare praesumpserit..."* (If anyone should dare to alter this...).

For he too one day — long before succeeding him or dreaming of ever becoming his successor — had paid homage there to the sacred relics; he too, as a Roman priest, had said Mass at his altar; and in the verses of the hymn thereon inscribed had invoked in him the great Legislator of the Church's worship,

> *Nemo, beate Pontifex,*
> *intensiore robore,*
> *quam tu, Superni Numinis*
> *promovit in terris decus,*

> (No one, O Holy Pontifex,
> Has more than you excelled in zeal
> To foster here on earth below
> The glory of the most high God.)

the Defender of Christianity,

> *Ausisve fortioribus,*
> *avertit a cervicibus*
> *quod christianis gentibus*
> *iugum parabant barbari...*

> (For by his daring mighty deeds
> He turned aside the servile yoke
> With which the rude barbarians sought
> To bind the necks of Christian folk...)

Fortunately, just then one of his secretaries came to distract him with a request for the text of the telegram to be transmitted to Tirana. They were now over the Adriatic and Albania was the first country after Italy that they would fly across. Russia approached in advance, had refused permission to fly over her territory, which for a number of years now had included Yugoslavia, Bulgaria and Roumania.

Then, singly or in groups, the members of his party who had not yet been able to pay him their respects began to visit his compartment. The civilian male attire which they all wore made it difficult at times to distinguish between ecclesiastics and laymen, or sometimes between men and women; so much so that the Pope, his attention being distracted, actually addressed as 'Cardinal' a member of the fair sex in the person of Adriana Zarri, well-known theologian and journalist, co-editor with Raniero La Valle of the *Nuovo Osservatore Romano*: — and though he apologised and smiled over his slip, he fell into a similar mistake just a moment later by calling a longhaired young bishop *'Signorina'*.

The rings which some wore and others did not were of little help or served at most to distinguish between married and single. For "anti-triumphalism" and the cult of the proletariat had induced most prelates to do without one, whilst episcopal rings in any case were now exactly like ordinary marriage-rings, and in the Papal retinue there was no lack of married ecclesiastics.

Amongst them was Monsignor Musante (no longer "ex") with his wife. She was his assistant at the Curia in the department dealing with cases of priests who had been rejected or driven out by their flocks because of their marriage and now needed a job, or of those priests who were looking for a job in order to get married.

There were also a number of divorcees among the clergy on board. These, it is true, had been accepted with reluctance by the Pope. For if he had ended up by giving in on the question of priestly celibacy — letting it fly out of that window of "ordination for married men advanced in years"[6] conceded to the wife-advocating Dutch bishops after he had locked the door on it with his *Sacerdotalis Coelibatus* — yet he had stood firm and Pope-like on the indissolubility of marr-

31

iage; and he would have liked there to be no scandal from priests, at least in this, after that given by certain of them who had followed Luther's example in marrying nuns, or had had nuns for bridesmaids in ceremonies performed by bishops.

Luther, now that we have made reference to him, no longer represented for Catholics, and especially for the clergy, the arch-heretic that the Church had excommunicated in the famous Bull of Leo X. In the name of "oecumenism" Rome had accepted the appeal of the Federation of Lutheran Churches, backed as it was by the Episcopal Conferences of many countries; and not only was his sentence of condemnation repealed, but the Protestant sects now had apologies offered them by those whom their founder had described as, amongst other things, "stupid cattle and disgusting pigs", whose Church, "that swinish Church" of theirs, was but "their sty".

The name of Luther was now held in high esteem — and properly so — by the "post-Council" or, as they themselves preferred to say, the "pre-Council" Catholics. A new Council was imminent. Vatican III, or Geneva I, as many wished it to be, would put the finishing touches to Vatican II. It would abolish, for instance, any distinction of "churches" between those who, believers or not, were followers of the "pure Gospel". And this was quite right; for it was impossible not to see in Luther the inspirer, the teacher, and the precursor of all the main reforms already enacted or now in course of preparation in the fields of theology and discipline, as also in that of a liturgy which was still Catholic in name: the rejection of priestly celibacy; abolition of abstinence, of indulgences, of devotion to Our Lady and the Saints; suppression of individual confession; elimination of Latin and Gregorian Chant; the "priesthood of the laity"; and equality between religions — to name only a few out of many, were all to be found among the "ninety-five theses" put up by this renegade on his Wittemberg church door. His "catechism" had served, too, as model for the Dutch one, now translated and gradually adopted in other countries in place of that of Pius X, with none of the modifications which the Pope had suggested in order to eliminate al least its most obvious heresies.

In the Pope's party a place had also been rightly reserved for the Archbishop of Florence, Monsignor Mazzi, successor to Cardinal Florit. He had been elected by the Priests' Council, that organ which in each "Diocesan Community" acted in democratic collaboration with the Lay Council for the nomination of bishops, in the same way as the Parish Council saw to the appointment of parish priests. This fact, however, had not given him nearly as much satisfaction as that of seeing raised to the status of accepted doctrine what his predecessor had felt bound to condemn as unsound. "The New Catechism", when being presented to the Press by Monsignor Del Monte, [7] head of the Italian National Catechetical Office, had indeed been declared to be "derived in great part from the famous Dutch catechism and in equal measure from the "Catechism of the Isolotto", including in its teaching for the first time such questions as peace, liberty, social justice, political involvement, international co-operation, development", and so on: things for all of which the famous Florentine agitator had fought alongside the Communists with the backing of comrade priests and prelates, such as the present President of the Italian Episcopal Conference, Cardinal Baldassarri, former Bishop of

Ravenna, famous in his own right for the approval given to a Protestant Bible and for his open-mindedness on the matter of divorce.

This same Monsignor Mazzi, for his merits aforesaid, was a member of the executive committee of the Italian Episcopal Conference, now "democratised" and more important than ever in view of the reforms in preparation on the election of the Pope. These had been proposed by Cardinal Suenens of Belgium and adopted by the Bishops' Synod, a permanent advisory organ by now chiefly responsible for the Pope's decisions. Technical details were still being worked out, like the electronic system of vote-counting, the use of a siren in place of the old-fashioned column of smoke, and the choice of language or languages — naturally with the exclusion of Latin — for transmitting the simple "communiqué" which would replace the emphatic "*Habemus Papam!*" of the past.

It had been the Pope's express wish to have Cardinal Suenens beside him on the first occasion he had appeared on the Vatican balcony in his white Papal soutane. It had been as though he were saying: Here is my programme! And ever since then the Cardinal had done his utmost to diminish Papal power. He it was who, as a first step, had "democratised" the process of succession to the Papal throne; it was what was defined by the lay Press as the most revolutionary of the innovations. The newspapers had come out with headlines like *Ecclesiastical General Staff* and *Civil Constitution of the Clergy*. They foresaw in this, in the matter of Papal primacy, a stage further towards Place de la Concorde and its twenty-first of January; for it was his proposal which vested in the Episcopal Presidents of the Bishops' Conferences, indirectly deriving from "the people", the election of "the Bishop of Rome". This, in fact, for some time now, was how he was referred to in the Pontifical Directories. There was no mention of those other Papal titles — Vicar of Christ, Successor of the Prince of the Apostles, Sovereign Pontiff of the Universal Church, Patriarch of the West, Primate of Italy — which Paul VI had himself laid claim to and listed in an outburst of righteous but over-late indignation — of resolute but short-lived resistance to the moving spirits of Vatican II who, in their "collegiality", had aimed at and eventually succeeded in making him little more than a *primus inter pares*.

The Synod, and therefore the Pope, was now on the point of accepting a Protestant proposal which would make him not so much *primus* as *one of many*. It would put him on the same level as the heads of those three hundred "churches" forming the Lutheran Oecumenical Council, self-defined as Christian, which was to say, believing, no matter how, in Jesus Christ, but not in the single Church He had founded: "churches" which hitherto the real church had considered as tendrils separated from the true Vine, and destined thus to wither and to die.

An affirmative reply had been given to the question which they had formulated and which the Pope had re-stated when he addressed their representatives in the City of Calvin during his visit to them as an uninvited but acceptable guest, on June 10th 1969: "Will the Catholic Church become a member of the Oecumenical Council?"[8]

This visit, this journey from Rome to Geneva, had in truth seemed so venturesome an act that even Cardinal König — and one could hardly say more — referred to it in the progressive Catholic newspaper

35

La Croix [9] as an outstanding event, and wrote: "John XXIII would perhaps have hesitated to act with such courage".

The Pope had indeed hesitated over this particular point, even though inclined as usual to follow whomsoever was advising him — in this case Cardinal Willebrands, worthy successor to the "well-loved Cardinal Bea". He had replied neither yes nor no, but had said "not yet", putting off till later what seemed to him something not to be discarded but only to be considered as premature: "We do not think that the question of the participation of the Catholic Church in the Oecumenical Council is sufficiently mature for one to be able or willing to give a positive answer. The question still remains in the field of hypotheses".

It was a hypothesis accepted as a certainty by the Protestants, and Pastor Van den Heuvel, one of the organisation's leaders, bluntly asserted: [10] "In five years the Catholic Church will ask for admission to the Oecumenical Council".

But it was also a hypothesis which filled Catholics with bewilderment and dismay. They remembered what that other Paul, the Apostle, had said: *Quae societas luci ad tenebras, aut quae pars fideli cum infideli?"* (What has light got in common with darkness, or the believer with the unbeliever?). They were also bewildered and dismayed, hurt and humiliated, at the manner in which their Pope had been received by these people in their temple. From the moment of his entry he had been made to understand that he was there on the same footing as themselves, merely the head of another "church"; there was no applause, no kind of special consideration, no seat apart, no dispensation from getting up and going to the common microphone to speak; the Pope with a little sheet of paper in his hand, precisely like the others, answering together with the others those prayers which they read out in turn on behalf of their various "churches", in English... in Dutch... in German... in all their representative languages, and never once in his, in the "Catholic language", the "Church's own language", — never once in Latin, not even when it was the turn of the Catholic, Cardinal Willebrands, to recite the prayer.

Catholics had then witnessed with further dismay, in the complacent report published in the Pope's honour by the *Osservatore Romano*, observations such as the one made by the Viennese newspaper [11] Paul VI... rarely made the Sign of the Cross", an educated way of saying he never made it at all. "The Pope made visible efforts not to seem out of place among people with outlooks different from his own. This was greatly appreciated by a public composed of many religions and many nationalities". With like dismay they read an *Osservatore Romano* report [12] in which "Pastor Vissert't Hofft, President of the Oecumenical Council, in eulogising Paul VI, made this criticism of Pius XII: "This visit will constitute a noteworthy date for us... *And the event is so much more noteworthy when we consider that as recently as 1954, on the occasion of the Plenary Assembly of the Oecumenical Council of Churches at Evanstone (U.S.A.), the Catholic Church had avoided any contact whatsoever"*. This availability on the part of Pope Montini, the Pastor continued, — and the *Osservatore Romano* did likewise, as it marked it up in his favour — was in such contrast to the intransigence of Pope Pacelli, that some people considered it excessive: "some Protestants and also certain Catholics, still maintain an attitude of reserve towards the Oecumenical movement, considering it to be too precipitate and to go too far". Which was a way of saying, respectfully: "Come right along, Peter, but... not too fast".

Peter, however, in his talks with the Protestants, as in his address on the same occasion to the Conference of the I.L.O., the Marxist-Masonic Labour Organisation, had this prudent conduct well in mind. For him too an excessive impetuosity had no part in that "spirit of *sound* oecumenism, primary condition of any fruitful contact" which should, as he then said, animate "both one side and the other", and be "open to every possibility of collaboration in fields where, even now, common action seems feasible and desirable: for instance, in the sphere of charity and in the quest for peace among the nations". But his whole heart was in the words, in the sigh, with which he concluded his speech: "Could We only be, as We so greatly desire, the pilgrim of reconciliation".

In this spirit, with this same desire, was he now flying in the great supersonic aircraft across the country which once was that of Scanderbeg, mighty champion of the faith, and which now lay beneath the rule, red in its flag and red with the blood it had shed, of one of the faith's fiercest enemies and persecutors... The reply from the head of the Albanian government to Paul VI's message of greeting from the sky above Tirana had been both prompt and courteous; and it too spoke of peace.

Between Moscow and Peking

It was for a number of reasons that Albania had unhesitatingly given her consent to the head of Vatican City for flight across her territory on his way to China.

First and foremost, a refusal would have been impossible, since it would have constituted an insult to Mao, on whose side she had ranged herself and by whom she had therefore been protected ever since the first clash between Moscow and Peking.

To China, and to the advisability for Russia not overly to provoke China, she owed whatever independence she had in the new political-territorial order that had emerged from the struggle between the two Communist giants for possession of the Euro-Asiatic Continent. China was a rival now in possession of all the nuclear weapons and with a population which, as Mao had boasted, "could still stand on its feet with seven hundred million people even after squandering in war as much as the entire population of Russia"; and Russia, constrained to hand over without a blow most of Siberia, where before she had held out successfully on the Ussari over a small fragment of it, humiliated now and depleted as she was in the East, had made up for it in the West by the military occupation of the Balkans. Yugoslavia had thus paid for her old sin of rebellion, even during the lifetime of Tito, who had perished by falling down a crevice on the Carso whilst fleeing from the gallows that his former overlords had prepared for him. Little Albania, however, had been able to taunt the Soviet warriors who, coming through Macedonia and Dalmatia, had reached her frontiers. They had been extremely careful not to overstep, them precisely because of the respect, not to say fear, which they had for a guardian whose prestige and power had waxed so tremendously after she had swallowed the whole of South-East Asia.

In her application for membership of the United Nations, Greater China had continued, none the less, to encounter the opposition of the Americans — still present and firmly established in Formosa after their withdrawal from the mainland — but this battle too, at diplomatic level, had been won thanks to the support of one of the latest and most authoritative members of the organisation, to wit, Vatican City. The Mao faction in the Vatican had got the better of the Muscovite one, and, having grasped the rudder of Peter's barque, was now steering it with the firm hand of one who was sure both of course and destination. This was a further reason why the *Ma-Ma* with the Pope on board could now wing its way across the *Eagle's Nest* flanked by a squadron of planes which had met it over the Adriatic and would accompany it, as a guard of honour, as far as the frontier of Greece.

This trip, this open alignment of the Vatican on the side of Peking, in the fight for world dominion between the two Communist capitals, had greatly irritated the Soviet leaders, as was shown by their refusal to let the aircraft fly over any countries under their control. It was also having consequences of a religious nature which had caused the Pope much unhappiness. Acting unilaterally and by government command, the Russian

Church had in fact broken off the "dialogue" initiated at the behest of Rome for the purpose of attempting re-union. This was the only one so far which had seemed at all possible to Paul VI, despite all his pains to "open doors", "build bridges" and remove obstacles on every side in his pursuit of that "sound oecumenism" — even if this, it must be confessed, sometimes gave the impression of putting more emphasis on the noun than on its qualifying adjective.

The Moscow Patriarchate had already done some backing away, questioning the orthodoxy of certain Roman innovations that were in conflict with ancient and venerated traditions which hitherto had been held in common. They appeared to smack more of Protestantism than of Catholicism, and were for this reason alone repugnant to the Most Holy Synod. And it was as the plane was leaving the sky of Greece and speeding above the Aegean that the radio in its news bulletin gave a piece of information referring to this which disturbed the august traveller considerably. Denouncing for its own part the agreement which permitted the Orthodox faithful to receive Communion at Catholic services and vice versa, the Patriarchate forbade its followers to indulge in this practice any longer, — not so much because of the dislike and disdain engendered by the "inter-Communion" which, after the decision of the Dutch Pastoral Council, had become general between Catholics and Lutherans, but because a more attentive examination of the text of the Mass current in the Roman Church since 1969 gave grounds for denying or at least casting serious doubts upon the validity of the Consecration. All the moreso since the Lutheran outlook by which the Catholic clergy themselves had become so widely infected gave the faithful no certainty whatever that what was absent, or was anyhow ambiguous in the words, was at least present in the intention of the celebrant.

Just then the voice on the inter-com which drew attention to and commented on the places which the *Ma-Ma* was passing over made the announcement: "We are now passing Naupaktos, formerly Lepanto, famous because, etc...".

They were over the Gulf of Corinth, and the figure of Pius V, already called to mind by the words he had just listened to on the validity of the new *Ordo* which he, Paul, had not willed but yet had promulgated, rose proudly up again in his imagination. And the arm that was raised, as it was in Sarzana's monument in St Mary Major's, seemed no longer pointed against the Turks but once more against him, — repeating for him in its gesture the same tremendous threat: *Si quis autem hoc attentare praesumpserit...* (If any man should dare to alter...).

A few years of imposed "experiment", of enforced application of his *"lex orandi"* which substituted the four hundred-year old one of his great and holy predecessor, had more than proved the truth of what had all been foreseen and foretold. The New Order was nothing more than a new disorder, a cause of disunion among those who had always been united, and an obstacle to re-union with those who had been and still were separated. — *"Nemo quam tu..."* (No one more than you), and the words which had been used of his predecessor for his defence of the Faith now seemed turned against him in blame for just the opposite.

Nemo quam tu... To the cry of grief that had arisen from his own flock there was now added the reproach of others, of those among the others who had been nearest and who might most easily have come back.

42

Now they had withdrawn again, accusing the Church, in its link-up with heresy, of abandoning that stable doctrine on which Catholic and Orthodox had never been divided.

Nemo quam tu... And far from easing his pain, that voice hurt him still further as it recounted, hoping to give him pleasure, how he, Paul VI, had restored to the Turks with a gesture of peace and almost of reparation the flag which had been wrested from them by the Christians in the famous naval encounter that Pius V had blessed. There was only contumely nowadays for the "warlike and triumphalistic" words which, on October 7th 1571, he spoke from his balcony: "The battle is won. I see fluttering in the breeze, over the enemy flagship, the banner of Christ. My children, let us go and give thanks to Mary". A gesture of peace? Of reparation? In Turkey, as a matter of fact, people had been inclined to laugh at the gesture. The Turks themselves had learned to appreciate the Pope's share in the safe-guarding of that civilisation — Western or Christian, however it be called — of which they too enjoyed the benefits, and for which even they, after their own fashion, had to be grateful to Mary.

How many such "gestures" had there been since then. Gestures which, while failing to bring back the lost or attract those who stood afar off, had, as he had just this moment learned, driven off those who had been most close; and the eyes of Paul VI turned in desolation to the beloved statue standing there beside him on the table, whilst his lips whispered the invocation which the Pope of Lepanto had added to the Litanies in appreciation and gratitude for that victory which he had commended to Our Lady's intercession and aid.

"The Mao Mass"

"*Auxilium Christianorum, ora pro nobis!*" (Help of Christians, pray for us!). Paul had not the strength of his predecessor, but he had his love for Our Lady, and Our Lady, as it appeared to him, now responded to his prayer. He had just been about to call for Cardinal Bugnini, when the Cardinal, with a brief-case under his arm, came in of his own accord to speak to him.

In his hand he was holding some sheets of paper on which red and black lettering alternated; and the pleasure of a job well done was clearly visible on his features. It was the text of the "New Mass" in Chinese, transposed into European script so that the Pope could read it when celebrating during his sojourn in Peking; for it was natural to suppose that Mao would give his consent and provide suitable premises for this. Not of course that suitability would present much difficulty. There was the faculty provided by the 1969 *Instructio Tertia* and the relevant practice deriving therefrom, of celebrating outside of church ("*extra ecclesiam*)" wherever it proved most convenient — not excluding diningrooms, for instance, and the tables that therein were to be found (*in cenationibus aut supra mensam cibariam*) — even though it might in principle be deprecated "*quantum fieri potest*".

"There", he said, holding out the little sheaf of papers. "We have had it looked over from the language

45

point of view by the hostess. She speaks several languages, has studied in the West, ...and even knows Latin!" He smiled as though at something curious, or strange and anachronistic, and then laughing outright he added: "She even said, this Chinese girl, that Latin as a sacred language seemed to her more beautiful!". The Pope lowered his eyes, neither laughing nor smiling, so he continued: "Anyhow, she has made some suggestions which seemed to us sensible and we have given them due consideration. She observed, for instance, that in Chinese the word for blood has a distasteful, vulgar connotation, and so we have altered that".

"By leaving the word in Latin, *sanguis?*"

"No, of course not, but by simplifying the formula: "the Body of the Lord" instead of "the Body and Blood", since the latter is included in the former and therefore there is no question of endangering orthodoxy... On the other hand, we have added something on... something which will make even Mao feel like coming to Mass", and he explained after laughing over the humour of it: "We have put into the liturgy of the Word and into the prayers of the faithful some extracts from his *Thoughts* and, among the inter-epistolary verses we have included some verses from his own poetry..."

Beginning to have his doubts as to whether this was, in fact, giving any pleasure to the Pope, in whose mixed expression amazement seemed to play the leading role, the Prefect of the Department for Divine Worship quoted part of Article 38 of the Liturgical Constitution "*...legitimis varietatibus et aptationibus ad diversos coetus, regiones, populos relinquatur*" (It may undergo legitimate variations or adaptations to different groups, regions or peoples): and since the

46

Pope's face still displayed doubt, the Cardinal played on that particular key which he knew for certain would have the desired effect on the mind of his hearer.

"Mao and the Chinese", he said, "will most certainly be grateful to us, and this will be yet another triumph for the oecumenism which Your Holiness, rightly, has so much at heart. — A triumph", he added, alluding to the news bulletin, "constituted by an opening on the Asiatic front, which will recompense us for the losses sustained, so to speak, by the closing down of the Russian one. A thousand million Buddhists are well worth the odd million Orthodox — even including the Greek ones who have never forgiven us for cutting out the *Kyrie eleison* and are still in the sulks about it...". The Cardinal tried with another smile to prise a smile from the Pope too.

The Greek government though not refusing the fly-over permit, had not in fact replied, as the government of Albania had, to Paul VI's telegram; and even if this was due, as it was reasonable to suppose, to political reasons based on the anti-Communism of Athens and to the consequent tension existing between there and Peking, Cardinal Bugnini was willing to believe, or pretended to believe, that there were also religious motives, and more precisely Orthodox resentment — shared, it must be said, by the Catholics of the region — for the complete exclusion of Greek from the Mass and from the entire "reformed" liturgy.

The combination of Greek, Hebrew and Latin (*Amen... Kyrie... Christe*) was a reminder of the trilingual inscription proclaiming the Kingship of Christ which Pilate had had placed over the Cross. In that sacrifice offered on the hill of Calvary, of which the Mass, both the Orthodox and the Catholic one, was

47

the renewal, it still represented for Catholics and Orthodox alike a continuing bond; whilst for the Jews it still represented a call to unity of sacrifice in unity of faith. The passion for reform had lacerated the common link, had broken down the bridge existing between East and West, all under the auspices of a "plurality" which tended of its nature to divide — *ut unum non sint* (that they be *not* one): that they be instead only a babel, a babel of which vernacular and dialect were the means, and also indirectly the end.

"In the same cart as the Russians", the Cardinal resumed as he opened his brief-case — and, still with the same smile, extracted further papers, "we can also put the English. I mean those English of the Anglican *Pilgrimage of Grace Movement* who wasted so much of our time back in 1970, soon after Your Missal had begun to be used. They are now returning to the attack under the leadership of that same Reverend Mr. Silk of London, still bearing the same petition, excepting that it carries more signatures, and that..."

"Petition about what?", asked the Pope, interrupting him.

"About what? ...It reached Willebrands, who passed it to us for information and comment the day before yesterday, on the eve of departure. Your Holiness naturally was up to the — had a whole host of other things to think of and to do, and so it seemed to us inopportune to disturb you by bringing this matter to your attention. They are Anglicans, as I have said, — and as you will possibly remember — who state that they are willing to enter the Church, to become Catholic, on condition that..."

"On condition that what?"

"On condition that... Well, here we are"... The

48

Cardinal took his glasses from his breast pocket, put them on, and said again as he read: "Here we are: they 'propose to re-establish in England the old Catholic faith for which the martyrs gave their blood', they declare themselves to be 'anti-Modernist and opposed to any theology tainted with Teilhardism or Modernism'. They think that 'the liturgy should not evolve, and *are in favour*' (the Cardinal underlined the passage by raising his voice) *'are in favour of the traditional Latin Mass which contributed to England's conversion to Christianity'*. They furthermore *'reject present-day oecumenism* and... deem it more important that people be converted than that the organisation of the Church and its rites be altered'. Devoted, as they assert themselves to be, to Our Lady, they inform us that it is their custom to 'join with members of the *Latin Mass Society* in reciting the Rosary for the return of England to the ancient faith, and that the Catholic Church *may preserve the Latin Tridentine Mass'* [13]. In other words," the Cardinal rapidly concluded, "they are asking the impossible". He said this with such a decided and resolute tone of voice, as he replaced his glasses and his papers, that the Pope appeared timidly to ask of himself rather than of him:

"Impossible?... Why impossible?"

"Why? Because", Cardinal Bugnini replied, "the period of dispensation from the New Order ended years ago in 1972, and to grant any more, to permit the use of Latin again, would be sheer nonsense — would be contrary to the unity of the Church... *"cum unum"* ...if I may use the Latin, *"cum unum in Ecclesia Dei Missae celebrandae ritum maxime deceat..."* (since it is most fitting that there be but one rite for celebrating Mass in the Church of God)".

Was it cynicism or lack of common sense? The Pope

49

— who knew these words only too well! — asked himself this. He raised his head as he asked it to look the Cardinal in the eye, and said with an unwonted and increasing emotion:

"But that is Pius V! It is the reason for which Saint Pius V promulgated the Roman Missal... *perpetuo valitura...* (by constitution valid forever and in all parts of the world). The unity of the Church! It was precisely for this reason that the Church always rigorously and jealously held on to Latin, the "pre-destined language", the "providential language", the "Catholic language", the "Church's own language", the "irreplaceable language". You well know whose these definitions are and how they were voiced in a variety of ways right on down and into Vatican II's *"Linguae latinae usus in ritibus latinis servetur"* (The use of the Latin language is to be maintained in the Latin rites); in fact, right down to the very person now speaking to you, Cardinal, who termed it the "angelic language", the "divine language", "consecrated Latin"; who compared it to a candle never to be let go out, even if, when it came to the point, and not without suffering for it, I then let others..."

"Others" meant *him*, especially him, and Cardinal Bugnini did not conceal his realisation of the fact.

"Your Holiness", he said, with respectful if rapidly diminishing embarrassment, "you also described Latin as an 'opaque diaphragm in place of clear crystal', and the image seems to me particularly apt. The vernacular means precisely that: clarity. No longer a *Deus absconditus*, a hidden God, even beneath the veils of a language that is angel..." (he was about to say "angelic" but stopped himself in time and said instead) "antique and beautiful like Latin; no longer *in nubibus* (in the clouds) but a God revealed, visible to all, great and small, learned and ignorant; and let every man see Him in his own way, form his own idea of Him, and so worship Him. Democracy, pluralism... that is the unity to which I intended to refer: unity in variety: *"in tot varietate linguarum"* (the same prayer for all in such great variety of languages), exactly as in your own Apostolic Decree *Missale Romanum...*"

He had won yet again; and returning without any pause to the original conversation, he continued: "This, then, is the Mass in Chinese. *In tot varietate linguarum*, and since we do not know how many hundreds of them they speak in China, we kept to the Mandarin of Peking, the official language, in which Mao's books are written. For us Latins it is not easy to pronounce, but if you like, if you think it useful to have a rehearsal. I can ask the hostess to come and help you with the reading of it".

The Pope gave his assent, and Cardinal Bugnini got up. He was pleased, for he had been afraid more than on previous occasions of "Montini's" hamletics and their effect on the stability of his reforming conquests. Then, as he was putting the papers that lay on the table back into his brief-case, he happened to brush against the statue of Our Lady and knock it over. He set it upright again with an apology and, still happily, went on his way. He was far from imagining what thoughts and disturbing memories had been reawakened by that trivial fortuitous incident. The Pope murmured again, and with an even greater dismay:

"Auxilium Christianorum, ora pro nobis!"

"Satan"

The hostess came in a moment later and began very politely to lend the Pope the help requested of her for reading the Mass in Chinese. Whilst making light of the not infrequent errors made by her august pupil because of the difficulty of the language — errors of pronunciation which sometimes produced words of completely different and curious meaning — she asked him, with innocent candour, why he was not saying it in Latin; and she added that it had always been said in Latin ever since the Catholic missionaries had first brought the Gospel to China. The Pope smiled.

"In Latin...!" he said. "I know that you are familiar with it, and I congratulate you. Do you also know something about...? I do not presume to ask you if you are a Catholic yourself, but do you happen to know anything at all about the Catholic religion?"

"I would say", she replied, "that rather than knowing something about it, I am not altogether ignorant of it. I have studied in Scotland, and lived in a hostel run by Catholic nuns; and though I am a Buddhist, and follower of the Lama Chogyam Trungpa living there in exile, I did sometimes take part in the ceremonies they held in their lovely chapel dedicated to the Virgin. The Mass, the ritual, the prayers, and the hymns... have ever since then had a place in my heart. And the

Virgin! — I remember, and shall always remember, the hymn which they used to sing to her... *Ave, Maris stella, Dei mater alma* (Hail Star of the Sea, Sweet Mother of God). No, I am not a Catholic; but I did want to be one. I was attracted, especially, by te beauty of it all. Our Lady! Even if I am not a Catholic, I pray to her and ask for her protection on all my journeys..." And taking from the breast-pocket of her uniform a small medal, she showed it to the Pope. He read the inscription which she told him she had had engraved around Our Lady's image... *Monstra Te esse matrem. Iter para tutum*... (Show thyself a mother. Make safe my path.). He kissed the medal devoutly and handed it back to her, as she went on: "The contacts which I had then also with Protestantism gave me nothing like this. And if I have never taken the step, if I have never become a convert to Catholicism, it is because when I went back some years ago to my old hostel in Scotland, I found everything changed: in the church all was cold, bare, without poetry; just as if the Catholics had become Protestants. A religion like that holds no attraction for us Chinese — not like the one which the missionaries from Rome taught to our fathers". And, with the same ingenuous frankness as before, she ended her earnest little speech by asking: "Why has all this been done? All the poems of Mao put together are not worth one verse of the hymns that I used to hear sung there — and that made me want to be a Catholic".

Why? Why was all this done? That, in fact, was the question which had been asked most frequently, inside and outside of the Church, since the beginning of his Pontificate. It was a question which, instead of dying down, had become more and more pressing and insistent as the changes followed on each other with mounting rhythm, until there came that day, November 30th, 1969, when a real wail of distress went up from some, a cry of incredulity from others, and everything had altered so completely that the Pope himself described it as the departure date for a "new epoch in the life of the Church"; — and since that time he had known no more peace.

Why? Why were these things done? He too asked himself the question yet again as the aircraft cleft its way through the Aegean sky, leaving Lepanto behind, but not the memory or the image of that Pope, with arm upraised as though in warning and in menace: *Nulli hominum liceat...! Si quis autem hoc attentare praesumpserit...* (let it be permitted to no man... If, however, anyone should dare to alter this...).

Why? He had put the question one day to a holy friar, sacristan of a monastery he had visited during his sojourn at Castelgandolfo, and the reply had been:

"Satan."

"Satan?"

"Satan", the friar had answered, making but this sole use of his dispensation from silence, and at the same time giving his questioner a look that had stopped any further question on his lips. — Returning to the villa, with that word and gaze still weighing upon him, the Pope had looked at and read again the message of Fatima: "Satan holds sway in the highest places, shaping the course of events. He will succeed in reaching the very summit of the Church... Cardinals will be ranged against Cardinals, Bishops against Bishops... Satan will march in the midst of their ranks... In Rome there will be great changes... Darkness will fall upon the Church... Satan wishes to possess himself of consecrated souls, suggesting too that religious life be brought abreast of the times..."

Satan... Satan... Satan. And it had been a welcome relief when he received that day the visit of one of his closest friends, the Cardinal President of the Revolutionary Liturgical Council, who had come to refer to him on the progress of the so-called Reforms... His friend had smiled benignly at the scruples of his "Montini", and to comfort him had shown him letters which hailed with enthusiasm all that was being done in the way both of destruction and construction, of undoing and re-fashioning. They were from bishops, priests and lay people.

As for those other letters of vehement dissent — by far the greater part, he could have informed him, had he felt inclined — he did not want altogether to hide their existence, but he put them down as the work of aesthetes, sentimentalists, and outdated conservatives; and indeed he succeeded in convincing him to such an extent that the Pope shortly afterwards came out with a contradiction of his own previous, repeated and impassioned pronouncements, such as the one with which he had brought the Council to a close: "To you, now, enamoured of beauty and working in her cause... The Church long since made common cause with you. You have built and adorned her temples, enshrined her dogmas, *enriched her liturgy*... Today as yesterday the Church has need of you and looks to you... This world in which we live needs beauty in order not to sink into depths of despair. Beauty, like truth, is what infuses joy into the hearts of men; it is the precious gift which is impervious to the ravages of time, that links the generations together and makes them one...".

Now he contradicted and condemned himself, using

some of his most pungent expressions against those who loved the beauty of the Church's liturgy [14]. "*Iis dicimus, qui, cum sint nimii vetustatis servandae cultoribus ob inane quoddam pulchritudinis studium... recens invectas mutationes acribus notavere verbis*" (We speak to those who, by reason of a certain foolish cult of beauty, are unduly attached to what has become out-dated and have recently made bitter attack upon the changes introduced). With the same emphasis with which yesterday he had praised them, today he bade the innovators pay no heed whatsoever to their criticisms and refuse to be restrained by them: "*...maximopere vitandum est ne pastoralium munerum renovationi inferantur impedimenta aut freni adhibeantur*" (no obstacles or checks must be allowed to hinder the renewal of pastoral duties).

It is true that these words were later given an officially unofficial twist, described by the *Osservatore Romano* as "its own" translation, which softened them and showed signs of second thoughts or indeed of a regret for the regret; but the innovators carried on in absolutely uninhibited fashion, with no need for spur or goad beyond their own tenacious determination.

Those who now considered the changes of the Reform to be the work of Satan saw clearly in them, above all, his pride. It emerged, that most characteristically Satanic sin, in the presumption with which men of little or no preparation presented themselves to pass judgment and contemptuous criticism on all that holiness, doctrine and genius, working for the glory of God and the elevation of souls, had created in harmonious collaboration and handed down through the centuries, until this our day. To Popes and saints, doctors and theologians, artists and poets, to men whose works were the joy and boast of the human race, these small, insignificant people had spoken thus: All of you have been completely and unutterably wrong: none of you ever understood a single thing. — They had addressed their mother and teacher, the Church, as follows: You have hitherto been plunged in ignorance; your teaching has been one big mistake; — and then, ripping out the page, flinging down the text-book, they had concluded: We are the men, the bright, the bold ones. Watch us now and see how it should have been done. Just for a start, begin all over again.

Begin all over again; Satan was again and especially recognisable in his unholy disrespect, in the steady, gradual — very gradual — job of degrading the Tabernacle, of eliminating decorum, reverence, and thus faith itself in the Blessed Sacrament. For, of course, This was very naturally the chief enemy, or indeed THE ENEMY, *tout court.*

These masters and ministers of grace, enlighteners and enlightened, were not content with demoting Him materially by turning their backs upon the Ciborium in order to celebrate facing the people, nor were they satisfied with having expelled Him from what because of Him had been known as the "High Altar". With an "Away with Him" from the new-type priests which rivalled in its fury that with which their earlier counterparts had called out to Pilate, they had shut Him up, segregated Him, not just "*in medio altaris minoris*" (in the centre of a side-altar), but "*etiam in alia ecclesiae parte*" (even in another part of the church), without altar and without any sign of "*ubi posuerunt eum*" (where they had laid Him).

Still unappeased, the reformers then worked on the *demythologising of the concept*, on bringing the devotion within reasonable limits. It was thus that at the altar we saw abolished genuflections and obeisances, elevations of the Host and certain silences, the kissing of the altar itself, and the respectful, upward glance of love. Now the precept was proscribed by which the celebrant was asked to say "*distincte, reverenter et secreto*" (distinctly, reverently and silently) the divine words of the Consecration; they were to be said instead "in a loud voice" and "like any ordinary piece of reading". Gone too was the following consequential rubric: "*deinceps pollices et indices non disiungit*" (henceforth he does not separate forefinger and thumb); an echo of the *ne pereant* (lest any be lost) of the Gospels which impressed upon priest and faithful the preciousness of even the tiniest fragment of that Bread that was no longer bread, of which the other was but the precursory image. With logical consistency, there was now no ablution for the fingers which had touched that Bread; and gone, of course, and derided too, was the imbibing of the water which had received those fragments, this being in their eyes nothing more than dirty water: *water which it is unhygienic to drink since it has server for washing of the hands.*

Gradually, very gradually, all of this; and meantime for the faithful it was proposed, suggested, counselled, permitted, imposed that they receive Communion standing up, thus following the example of the Protestant sects who thereby signified their denial that the Bread was anything more than bread, — a symbol to be honoured, not a reality to be worshipped. Communion eventually was refused with frowning disdain to any who, still wholeheartedly believing, desired by their action to give testimony to the words of St. Thomas: "*Deum meum Te confiteor*" (My God I do confess Thee to be).

Gradually, very gradually; and the number of Communions was lessened by forbidding Communion to be given outside of Mass. This, naturally, helped at the same time to insinuate the doubt expressed by the "new theologians" as to whether transubstantiation in the Host did not cease with the end of Mass and whether instead of transubstantiation it was not anyhow preferable and more correct to use "transignification" or "transfinalisation", with the obvious new significance which these new words carried with them.

The very number of Masses was reduced through the spreading of "concelebration". Sometimes as many as tens and hundreds of priests, partially, variously and ridiculously vested, took advantage of the permission granted by the *Instructio's* "*deficientia sacrorum paromentorum*" (lack of sacred vestments) and preferred the "*frequentior concelebrantium numerus*" (larger number of concelebrants) to the proper decorum of the rite. They crowded and jostled round the altar, or even stood among the faithful nearby, without book, without host or chalice of their own, dividing up the words and acts between them, pronouncing "This is My Body" with empty hands, or pointing a finger towards one of their number, the leading actor, or "principal concelebrant" as the *Instructio* called him, as though signifying that the "This" was the one who held Him in his hands on behalf of all the others.

The whole concept gradually, very gradually, had to be cut down to its right size; the "mystery" had to be demythologised, the sense of sacred and divine in the Eucharist had to be properly watered down. And so, just as the priest's prayers before and after Mass were removed from the missals, so the faithful were taught the inopportuneness not only of bothering about

Confession before Communion but of indulging in any thanksgiving afterwards. And anyhow, with the abolition of the *Placeat,* the last Gospel, and the Leonine Prayers after Mass, the speed with which the sacristy or the square outside were reached left time for swallowing down the Sacred Species and practically nothing else.

In the same spirit of anti-devotionalism, the traditional Expositions of the Blessed Sacrament were discouraged, and their frequency, duration and mode of actuation diluted. That of the Forty Hours was still tolerated (*"fieri potest"*) but for a lesser number of hours; whilst, though the throne for the Blessed Sacrament was tolerated also (*"thronus adhiberi potest"*), the injunction was made that it be not too high (*"et caveatur ne sit nimis elevatus"*); whilst, to encourage prayer (*"ad intimam orationem alendam"*) we were offered *"lectiones ex Sacra Scriptura"*, that is to say, the usual Protestant Bible Readings.

Tolerated too, rather than permitted — and still less recommended, was that most grandiose of Eucharistic manifestations, the ancient, universal Corpus Christi procession with its incorporation of those sublime hymns that angels themselves might well have dictated to the Angelic Doctor. — Not merely insensitive but actively hostile to certain human values, as they were, the reformers had fleetingly and reluctantly allowed this tradition to survive amid the ruins of so many others, but with a "but" attached, with a "however" that seemed a suggestion to sacrifice it. They passed its fate on to the bishops: to the docile bishops who, among so many other things, had driven out Latin from the Church despite the Council's deliberate and solemn stipulation; who had abolished the Regulations; who — thoughtful for the "exigencies of traffic" (as they had been not to disturb the tranquillity of worthy citizens by pastoral visits) had ordered private removal of the dead from house to church, without priest or prayers. "*Ordinarii tamen loci est iudicare cum de opportunitate, in hodiernis rerum adiunctis... huiusmodi processionum...*" (however, it will rest with the Bishop of the diocese to decide on the desirability of these processions in modern conditions).

Thus ran the *Instructio*; and, in the spirit of "modern conditions", the more up to date, more "anti-triumphalist" bishops considered it equally unsuitable to practise this manner of honouring the Blessed Sacrament. They either abolished the Corpus Christi procession altogether or curtailed it, with no thought for the feelings of the faithful, to whose happy participation reference had been made in a solemn Pontifical document: "*...in processionibus frequentissimi populi laetitia circumferendo...*" (bearing the Blessed Sacrament in procession to the joy of the assembled people). — It had been considered one of the great, open manifestations of our faith, an example of the veneration in which the Church had always held the "*ineffabile donum*" (the priceless gift) she had received from "Her Bridegroom, Christ". And as such it could only therefore be detested by the spirit of detestation, who saw in it — THE ENEMY.

Sadness and Boredom

"The Catholic Church offers supreme worship to
the Sacrament of the Eucharist not only during the
Mass, but also outside of its celebration, preserving
the consecrated Hosts with the utmost diligence, offering Them to the solemn veneration of the faithful,
bearing Them in procession for the joy of Christian
people..."

In this fashion Paul VI had spoken out against all
the deviations and aberrations of the innovators on
that holiest and most august "truth of faith", in the
most admirable of his encyclicals, his *Mysterium Fidei*.
This, along with his *Professio Fidei* and *Humanae Vitae*
had marked him as the truly elect of the Holy Spirit,
the Vicar of Jesus Christ, the successor of Peter and
continuer of his work — without any of the human
fallibility of Simon.

Firm in his re-iteration of truth — of the "sound
doctrine" taught by all his predecessors — he had
shown himself to be no less firm in the rejection of
error, whether in old, new, or renovated form, beginning with that concerning the Mass. The Reform was
the product of a Council, Vatican II, whose "innovators", though only recently condemned by the Pontiff
who had called the Council, had still taken over the
running of it from the very outset. — It was only then

beginning to take its first steps, but even these showed an orientation so much at variance with the straight path of faith as to perturb that faith's Custodian. "If the Sacred Liturgy occupies first place in the life of the Church", he said, "the Eucharistic Mystery is in turn the heart and centre of the Sacred Liturgy, inasmuch as it is the living fountain which purifies and strengthens us so that we live no longer for ourselves but for God, and through it are kept together in the closeknit bond of charity". With bitterness he then added: "There are not wanting, however, in this matter with which We are dealing, motives for grave pastoral concern and anxiety, regarding which the awareness of Our apostolic duty does not permit Us to remain silent". The first of these motives for anxiety which he deplored concerned the Mass, the reformers' Mass, and their exaltation of its "communal" nature: "it is not in fact licit... so to exalt the so-called community Mass as to take importance from the private Mass".

No indeed, for it had much less relevance to Catholic Communion than to Marxist Communism, and would lead with gradual speed, as it did, to a kind of collective Eucharist devotion, and in general to religious practice that was dry, formalistic and mechanical, turning the faithful into soulless robots without a spark of personal involvement. This was something of which, though still willing to hope, he had been prophetically afraid: — "In order therefore that the hope, raised by the Council, of a new light of Eucharistic devotion... be not frustrated and choked by the seeds of false opinions that have already been scattered, we have decided to speak..."

The fear was justified; and it was to be himself who would eventually highlight the evolution, he who would recognise in the undoubted and progressive "diminution of spiritual life" the failure of "communal" prayer, as he did in a talk of his in 1969[15], dedicated entirely to the "need for *returning* to personal prayer: to all those forms of prayer which the Church's religious practice has taught and instilled into us". He gave specific examples: — "like the Rosary, the Way of the Cross, meditation, adoration of the Blessed Sacrament, examination of conscience, spiritual reading". — And to illustrate how far removed all that was from the ideas of the "innovators" we need look no further than the Rosary: the Rosary which Pius XII had blessed and indulgenced as a means by which so many people might fruitfully participate "in the Eucharistic Sacrifice, and enjoy its benefits, whilst piously meditating on the mysteries of Jesus Christ[16]". Now it was forbidden; now the "new priests" hunted it out, forcing its devotees to conceal their beads, or else confiscating them and holding them up to public ridicule. Nor was this the only evidence of relationship and common outlook between the "community concept" and Communism when in power.

And as the "communal" aridity continued and grew, with deleterious effects "even among the clergy and religious", the Pope shortly raised his voice again: "Prayer today is falling into desuetude[17]", he said. Could it be a consequence of the Reform? "Yes", one knows he would have liked to say, — or would have said, had he been allowed. But he was not, and so he said it only by implication, using a "but" which had all the validity of a "because": "Liturgical community prayer is beginning once more to spread... but we must deplore the fact that personal prayer is diminishing, thus threatening the liturgy itself with inner impoverishment, with external ritualism, with practice that is purely formal. Religious sentiment itself may die away if there is lack of a two-fold characteristic which is indispensable to it: it must have an interior and an individual quality. ...Are we but empty souls, despite our being Christian, souls that have lost themselves, forgetful of the mysterious, inexpressible encounter that God deigns to provide for our filial and rapt colloquy with Him — precisely within ourselves?" One seems to hear the voice of Christ speaking through His Vicar: *Populus hic labiis me honorat; cor autem eius longe est a me* (This people honours Me with its lips; but its heart is far from Me).

"Inner impoverishment", "external ritualism", "purely formal practice", colloquy with God outside of ourselves instead of "within ourselves...". These are, in reality, the features and the effects of "communal" devotion: a "switched on" devotion, all words, as irksome as certain insipid theatrical productions in Plautus's day of which he wrote ..."*Lumbi sedendo et aures auscultando dolent*" (Listening to these is as hard on the ears as it is on the seat).

Irksomeness, sadness and *boredom,* where before — both in its anticipation and its realisation — lay all that made up the Christian's holy-day. Sadness for those who, *from the waters of Babylon,* from the exile of their solitude, remember the songs of Sion; boredom for those who, having accepted the yoke as legitimate and good, believing or wishing to believe in *Egypt and the Assyrians,* accept their religion as well and adopt their sacred songs, but find no solace in them for their hearts: hearing, perhaps, beneath the vaulted roofs of churches no longer theirs, perhaps not even materially theirs, inasmuch as they have been reformed, despoiled, made "poor" and "functional" instead of beautiful and holy — hearing the lament of the prophet for a Jerusalem which is no longer Jerusalem: *Quomodo obscuratum est aurum, mutatus est color optimus, dispersi sunt lapides Sanctuarii...* (How is the gold tarnished, changed the peerless colour, and scattered the stones of the Sanctuary...). — And it may be that they too will ask, but in apprehension, what Clodoveus, the barbarian king, asked in ecstasy of the Bishop, St. Remigius, who had converted him. Amid the singing, music, lights and liturgical rites of Christmas he crossed the threshold of Rheims Cathedral for his baptism, and asked: "Is this the Paradise you promised me?"

Is this the Paradise? So many people have asked themselves this all down the centuries, whether already participating in it *ab intus*, or looking at it, listening to it, envying it from its threshold until the day when they too were eventually drawn to enter it. They were attracted perhaps by the verses or notes of one of its hymns, at times more persuasive than any reasoning, like a "note of the eternal poem" that has sounded for them, by God's grace, in their souls. *Pulchra es et decora, filia Ierusalem!* (Beautiful art thou and fair, O daughter of Jerusalem!) — Joyous as had been the cry, throughout the centuries, of those brought up within it or of those who had come to enter it, so equally desolate now was the plaintive questioning both of those abandoning it in their failure to recognise it any longer as theirs, and of those who sadly retraced their steps when they had been on the point of crossing its threshold. *Haeccine est urbs perfecti decoris, gaudium universae terrae...?* (Is this the city of surpassing splendour, the joy of all the earth...?).

No, it is not. But what is true is that for the first time in two thousand years the fount of conversion has dried, and wells up no longer. And he who allowed this thing to come to pass, who, in spite of all his app-rehension, let the children go forth in tears and the questing stranger be repelled, he who failed to check the foe, within and without, from destroying the Para-dise's surpassing splendour, today cries out in vain at the devastation surrounding him, vainly repeats the prophet's appeal: *Ierusalem, Ierusalem, convertere...!* (Turn again, O Jerusalem...!).

Apprehensive certainly he had been, but not to this extent. How could he be, when after having co-operat-ed in drawing it up, he had approved the Council's definition of Divine Worship? With apostolic fervour this document had paraphrased in prose the Dedica-tion hymn... "In the earthly liturgy we participate, by anticipation, in that celestial one which is celebrated in the holy city of Jerusalem, towards which we journ-ey as pilgrims, wherein Christ sits at the right hand of God as Minister of the sanctuary and of the true tabernacle; together with all the ranks of the heavenly hosts we sing to the Lord the hymn of glory; in remem-bering the Saints with veneration, we hope to find place alongside them; and we await our Saviour, the Lord Jesus Christ, our life, until He shall come, and until we appear with Him in glory".

No, not to this extent. Now the "heavenly armies", the "heavenly hosts", and the choirs of angels were by reason of their "militaristic" and "triumphalistic" connotation — to seem odious to the reformers and therefore, shall we say, expendable. They proclaimed their elimination from the Mass and from the Litanies, but did so in language appropriate to saboteurs, to dynamiters: "Let the Thrones, Principalities and Powers be blasted out". The Saints received a similar fate and were likewise outlawed. The Apostles themselves were expunged, "blasted out" of the Mass, out of the Canon where, each named personally, they had been ranged side by side as in some sublime Leonardi painting, and at the moment of Consecration recalled almost visually the Last Supper, the first Holy Mass. The Consecration itself was threatened with a reform in keeping with the greatest Reform, that of Luther.

Not thus far had the Pope thought they would go when he gave the signal and started the race on March 7th, 1965. It was not in this sense that he had defined that Sunday as "a memorable date in the history of the Church"; on the contrary, only a short time later he issued this warning to those who had thus understood it, who showed too soon what were their real thoughts and intents: "Some have allowed themselves to fall into error over the new directives and have shown themselves more ready to destroy than to preserve and develop. But no: the Council is not to be considered as a kind of cyclone, a revolution upsetting ideas and traditions and permitting rash and unthinkable novelties. No, the Council is not a revolution: it is a renewal."

It is not a revolution? It was not intended to be one?- Or it was not considered to be one? — Which? When Louis XVI made an analogous assessment of the excesses which followed his Constitution, saying "It is a vast upheaval", the Duke of Liancourt made answer, "No, Sire; it is a vast revolution". And the Temple and the Place de la Concorde were at hand. — Similarly, the evidence of the ill done, of the devastation that contrasted so strongly with the hopes nourished, was rapidly making of March 7th a more and more "memorable date"; — and more and more did Paul VI feel all the bitterness of it. Deplorations and implorations were multiplied on his lips, but all of them in vain. "What is he worrying about?" asked the Jacobins of the Reform, and carried on with the work of suppression and destruction that was done in his name and with the authority of his seal.

These were things that were still valid, but used almost exclusively for the ratification of their decisions. "*Domine, quis credidit auditui nostro? et brachium nostrum cui revelatum est?*" (Lord, who has believed what we have heard, And to whom has our power been revealed?) And the faithful who still believed fervently in that *Tu es Petrus* (*Thou* art Peter), in *Tibi dabo claves* (To *thee* I will give the keys), in *Pasce oves* (Feed (*thou*) my sheep) — and wanted no part of any plurality — asked themselves in their passionate, jealous love for him, whether he really believed any longer in himself, or in his prerogatives and duties. They had no desire to have to distinguish repeatedly between Peter and Simon: between Peter, foundation-stone of the Church, Vicar of Jesus Christ, voice of the Holy Spirit, and Simon, frail, insecure, inconstant, *a man like ourselves*, one who contradicts himself by permitting what shortly before he had forbidden, or by forbidding what before he had permitted: who declares himself unable because of the love that is in him, "*pro benevolentia*", to grant a request which, if granted, "would be certain cause of weakness and of sadness throughout the entire Church of God": ("*Nolumus id permittere quod certe toti Ecclesiae Dei aegritudinem ac moestitiam afferat*" — a reference to the introduction of the vernacular in chanting the Office) [18], and who yet assents not only to its licitness but even to its enforcement on those reluctant to accept it; who desires Communion to be received whilst kneeling, but yet, out of deference to others, himself receives Communion standing up.

Nolumus-Volumus, Volumus-Nolumus... (We don't want to, we do; we do want to, we don't). And so, as an effect of this, one small example among so many others, in Rome we had the spectacle of the Pope, in accordance with the decrees of the Council, giving instructions that Masses be said and sung in Latin and in Gregorian Chant — "*...una alterave missa, sive lecta, sive in cantu, lingua latina celebretur. In eiusmodi missis cantatis gregorianae melodiae vel sacra poliphonia peculiari cura et studio proferantur*"[19] (...one or two Masses, either low Masses or sung, are to be celebrated in Latin. In these sung Masses Gregorian Chant or polyphonic music is to be rendered with special care and devotion), whilst his Vicar-General ordered that at Mass in those same churches, between the Gospel and the Offertory, public prayers be offered against those Catholics who desired and were still asking for "the return of Latin and Gregorian Chant". We may note in passing that they were described, in terms highly suited to the place, the act, and the moment — in extremely charitable terms, let us say, as: "rebellious, disorderly, disobedient and futilely nostalgic". Extraordinary terms, it must be admitted, since the rebellion was due to loyalty, the disorderliness to constancy, and their so-called disobedience derived from strict obedience to Pope and Council. Furthermore, if we care to make the point, they were acting in harmony with the very person who, as Vicar-General, had himself subscribed to the Pope's instructions[20] and who thus was emulating Dante's bizarre Florentine that tore himself to pieces with his own teeth.

And what of the Pope? The Pope begged, implored and deplored, but — whether because he was powerless or was unwilling to act otherwise — he let things take their course. It was not for nothing, not without significance, that now in Papal functions, even on the very anniversary of his coronation, the tiara was no longer placed on his brow, nor the *Tu es Petrus* sung in his honour. That "democracy" now established in the Church through "collegiality", the "Synod", and reaching right down to the lowest ranks of the hierarchy, operated at the top in its most inefficient civil form: "the king reigns but does not govern". The aborition of the triple crown helped to eliminate any thought or memory of monarchical rule, particularly that of an absolute one *ad iudicium Summi Pontificis* (reserved for judgment of the Supreme Pontiff).

Paul VI's personal aversion for the "sceptre", his abhorrence of the "rod", encouraged the boldness and effrontery of the innovators, resolved on destroying, on "blasting out" all things that had been there before their March 7th: "things", as one of them wrote in barbarous fashion, "which might have been the joy of baroque eyes"[21], not pausing to remember that among those "baroque eyes" were those of the Pope, who had spoken then and later of "a sacrifice... a sacrifice of inestimable price", of "a stupendous and incomparable heritage" that had been lost, and who, in his continuing eulogies, seemed bent on seeking the pardon of God and man for having abandoned it, or at anyrate for not having prevented its loss.

72

He was absolved in his own eyes by the faith he nurtured, despite repeated disillusions, in goodness as a form of government. He believed in the spirit of the Council,"his" Council of Vatican II, which he considered superior to all others — as he had not hesitated to infer by contrasting rather than comparing it with them. ..."In the past Council teachings regularly ended up by expounding and deploring some error and by condemning it with a classical *"anathema sit"* (let it be anathema); the didactics of Vatican II tend to throw into relief what it is fitting to praise, to appreciate, to do and to hope for. The Council, as we have said, is bent on doing good". [22]

No anathemas, no condemnations, therefore; and this was the reply given to the five hundred and thirty-two bishops from all parts of the world who in anxious alarm for "the rapidly collapsing situation" had declared amongst other things: "We reject all new interpretations of the Faith, which lead in effect to a falsification of Revelation. We reject any democratisation of the Church, which could only lead to revolution. We reject any ill-considered dialogue, giving the impression that everything today is open to discussion; and also any ill-considered attempt at modernisation which is contrary to the message of the Cross. We demand that the Church have the courage to exercise its judicial authority, and that once more, in the same spirit as the Apostle, she pronounce her anathema, in order that the spirit may be saved". [23]

No, no anathemas. This was also the answer given to a well-known Italian bishop who, speaking before his brethren gathered in general assembly, had said: "Courage is part of our ministry. Hesitation and doubt on those things that should be certain are not. Wolves must be treated as wolves. None of our sheep can be abandoned through any cowardice on our part. A conception of the priesthood based on merging in with the colours of the world, on perpetually yielding instead of fighting against the wolves, would only be betrayal. A betrayal, likewise, would be the avoidance of combat through accepting all the world's smoothness of thought and method and action. The abandonment of our sheep to bewilderment and slaughter would be a betrayal deserving the only title which Our Saviour reserves for cases of this kind: that of hireling!"[24]

No anathemas at any price. No facing up to the wolves, whether openly such or in sheeps' clothing; only goodness, goodness at all costs. In this spirit, in accordance with these same "didactics" there came about the abolition of the Index. So that quite licitly, without any attempt at censorship, there were now in circulation books of a "new theology" like *The Death of God* or *Satan is Dead;* there were "catechisms" of doubtful conformity, and books of a "new morality" which approved of Onan and justified or exalted Sodom, to the point of making it little less than a sacrament. Pius X's antimodernist oath was ridiculed in the name of "religious liberty" and exchanged, so long as it fitted the situation, for a species of anti-wife oath that was requested of priests.

Goodness in all things and towards everybody; and if there was to be any exception, if toughness and severity were to be exercised at all, then let us observe how and against whom it was to be done. Let us hear it as recounted in amazement by persons outside of the Church: by, for instance, Marcel Regamey, one amongst the many, who on January 10th 1970 wrote as follows in the *Nation Vaudoise*: "After Vatican II one might have thought that the use of the vernacular

74

would be authorised but not imposed, and so too with the Order of the Mass and the texts. It is not without amazement that we Protestants see the liturgical revolution in the Catholic Church imposed upon the generality of the faithful... The faithful have thus had wrested from them the concrete background against which their spiritual life was set and have had another one manufactured for them... Authority instituted to preserve and protect the deposit of faith cannot without being tyrannical prescribe, by means of that same authority, changes which are equivalent to a revolution. Thus, whilst it is being attacked from its foundations, *authority in the Catholic Church is being exercised in tyrannical fashion against its most loyal sons*".

These were the Catholics concerning whom the plane's radio, in mentioning the anniversary of the "liberation" of the ex-Portuguese African colonies, contemptuously recalled a famous pilgrimage to Rome: famous because of a certain refusal and a contrasting acceptance, by reason of which the announcer lauded "him who at this moment is flying towards the China of Mao"; but Paul VI winced as he listened, as though from a painful open wound that was being repeatedly disturbed.

The Bread and the Stone

He was already upset by another event that was doubly sad for him. The Holy Synod had demoted his friend, the Patriarch Athenagoras. Despite his great age, they had found themselves unable to overlook his approaches to a Catholic Church which had, amongst other things, down-graded devotion to Our Lady, cancelled from the calendar saints like St. Nicholas of Bari who were deeply venerated by the Orthodox Church, and had offered the hand of friendship to the exponents of atheism. — It was now cruel torture for him to have to listen to praise and hear the evocation of associations which had already so greatly humiliated him in far-off 1970:

"Angola, Guinea, and Mozambique are celebrating today, with a huge display of red flags, the anniversary of their liberation. They are honouring the heroes who fought for this, and they are remembering also those who, without taking up arms, gave their contribution to victory, if only by their moral support.

First among these is he who at this moment is flying towards the Greater China of Mao: who was not afraid, whilst the battle was raging, to receive and bless the leaders of the revolt — Marcelino Dos Santos, Agostinho Neto, Amilcar Cabral —: who braved the resentment of the Portuguese government and paid no heed to the cry of "scandal" raised by the whole conservative and reactionary world...".

This "scandal" was all the more striking because of the fact that on the previous day Paul VI had refused both audience and blessing to a large pilgrimage of Catholics who had come, with no small effort on their part, from a number of countries — even from as far away as America — to offer prayers on his behalf and to re-assert, on the feast of St. Peter, their profession of faith in the traditional Church. The Vatican newspaper itself had high lighted the episode by writing in justification of the audience which had been accorded: "The Pope, by reason of his mission, receives all those who seek the comfort of his blessing".

The Communist and progressive-Catholic press exalted this "event", rightly defining it as "historic". They gave it abundance of comment and published a photograph of Paul VI surrounded by those of the three revolutionaries.

"In all this", the radio continued, "the Pope was himself a revolutionary, for he showed a courage and foresight that completely out-distanced his predecessor Pope John; and it is because of this that, we repeat with respect, he is now on his way to China, determined to bring about between Communism and Catholicism an understanding like that already existing in what has been called the Italian "post-Council" republic: a real redemption of the people along the lines of *Das Kapital* and *Populorum Progressio*. This has already been reflected in the new proletarian community cult which honours human labor no less than it does...".

In order not to hear what he knew was coming next, a placing of the works of God and man on the same level, and being in any case deeply annoyed by what he had heard, the Pope brusquely switched off the radio. He was not, however, able to switch off in the same way the gnawing memory of what for all these years he had tried to forget: not so much the audience he had given, but the one he had refused.

The concession of the first audience had, by its contrast, emphasised the refusal, the cold, hard refusal of the second. And it was not the mental picture of his portrait in the *Unità*, for instance, which caused him most suffering now. (It had been duly displayed along with those of the three notorious killers referred to, and the pious had thought compassionately of "Christ upon the Cross"). It was less, even, the thought that there had been blood upon their hand-shake — including the blood of priests and nuns. What really hurt him now was the memory of those children of his kneeling in prayer on the stones between the circling arms of the colonnade in front of St. Peter's. — It was once written that these arms were "a symbol of the arms of the crucified Apostle". And it was there that they had knelt, on the square, during the night of the Pope's feast-day, June 29th 1970.

Filii tui de longe venient... (Thy children will come from afar...) — and some of them were indeed from afar, come to protest their love and to ask for a fatherly word of reassurance on the attempts then being made to undermine their faith as Catholics. There were people of all tongues, and they prayed beside the obelisk in one tongue alone, that of the Church — old and always new, perennial and pure, like water from a living spring. They prayed with the Church, for the Church, and for him: *Ut Ecclesiam tuam sanctam regere et conservare digneris... Ut domnum apostolicum et omnes ecclesiasticos ordines in sancta religione conservare digneris... Ut inimicos*

79

*sanctae Ecclesiae humiliare digneris... Ut cuncto popu-
lo christiano pacem et unitatem largiri digneris... Ut
omnes errantes ad unitatem Ecclesiae revocare et infid-
eles universos ad Evangelii lumen perducere digneris... Pro Pontifice nostro Paulo... ut te donante tibi
placita cupiat et tota virtute perficiat...* (That Thou
wouldst vouchsafe to govern and preserve Thy holy
Church; That Thou wouldst vouchsafe to preserve our
Apostolic prelate and all orders of the Church in holy
religion; That Thou wouldst vouchsafe to humble the
enemies of holy Church; That Thou wouldst vouchsafe
to grant peace and unity to all Christian people; That
Thou wouldst vouchsafe to recall all wanderers to the
unity of the Church and to lead all unbelievers to the
light of the Gospel; For our sovereign Pontiff Paul...
that by Thy grace he may both desire those things that
are pleasing to Thee and perform them with all his
strength). — And he listened as they prayed.

He listened to them praying from his room high up
in the Vatican, the only one showing light, the only
one in all the great building, one imagines, where vigil
was being kept; and where certainly there was no rest.
*Cum invocarem exaudivit me Deus iustitiae meae: in
tribulatione dilatasti mihi... Miserere mei et exaudi
orationem meam... Mirificavit Dominus sanctum suum:
Dominus exaudiet me cum clamavero ad eum... Sacri-
ficate sacrificium iustitiae et sperate in Domino... Su-
sceptor meus es tu et refugium meum: Altissimum
posuisti refugium tuum... Quoniam in me speravit lib-
erabo eum: protegam eum quoniam cognovit nomen
meum... Clamabit ad me et ego exaudiam eum: cum
ipso sum in tribulatione, eripiam eum et glorificabo
eum...* (God, guardian of my rights, Thou answerest
when I call, When I am in trouble Thou comest to my
relief. Now be good to me and hear my prayer — The

80

Lord works wonders for those He loves, The Lord hears me when I call to Him — Offer sacrifice in a right spirit and trust the Lord — My refuge, my fortress — You have made the Most High your dwelling — I rescue all who cling to me, I protect whomsoever knows my name — I answer everyone who invokes me, I am with him when he is in trouble. I will save him in distress and give him glory). It was thus that they prayed, chanting their Compline verse by verse in serene melancholy; and the petitions were like dagger-thrusts at his heart, at that heart which had refused to receive them, and had given to others — not to speak of what others! — the biblical bread, fish, and egg sought of him by his children. — He listened to them, in his unhappy vigil; and in the obsessive roar, the sinister winking of an aeroplane which at that moment was flying through the darkness above the Basilica, he seemed to sense a symbol of the demon that they were seeking for strength to fight against: *Scuto circumdabit te veritas eius, non timebis a timore nocturno... a sagitta volante in die, a negotio perambulante in tenebris, ab incursu, et daemonio meridiano*: (His truth will encompass thee with a shield, you will not fear the terror by night... nor the arrow that flies by day, nor the plague that prowls in darkness, nor the onset of the mid-day fiend): the demon that they were determined to resist, the "roaring lion", devourer of souls whom, "strong in faith", they were determined to withstand: perhaps the demon of whom it was prophesied at Fatima: "He will succed in reaching the very summit of the Church".

Serene they were in their melancholy, unwitting of his pain, — as though the verses they chanted in the night had no present relevance, no application to him: *Signatum est super nos lumen vultus tui, Domine:*

dedisti laetitiam in corde meo... in pace in idipsum dormiam et requiescam... Ipse liberavit me de laqueo venantium... (The light of Thy face is turned on us, O Lord: Thou hast given joy to my heart... I will lie down in peace and sleep will come to me... He has freed me from the snare of the fowlers...) — They prayed all through the night — they the unheard, the rejected, — for the Church and for him: *Te lucis ante terminum, rerum Creator, poscimus...* (Before the closing of the day, Creator, we Thee humbly pray...); and the sweetness of their prayer, the grandeur of their psalms, and the gentleness of their hymns was torment for him... Could he have, had it depended on his will alone, he would have flung open that half-closed window and, throwing out his arms towards them, he would have called to them: "Come!"

Unable to do more, he sank to his knees on the bare floor, and kneeling as they were doing on the hard stones of the square, he prayed all night along with them.

In his frailty, in Simon's human weakness, he was unable to do more; and there came to his mind the thought of an atrium, a maid-servant, and a dawn breaking — just as they were chanting down below: *Cedant tenebrae lumini. Et nox diurno sideri... Ut culpa quam nox intulit. Lucis labescat munere...* (Cleanse Thou the gloom, and bid the light Its healing beams renew; The sins which have crept in with night With light shall vanish too) — And thinking more of himself than of the people to whom he would speak the words, he wrote what he would say that day at the moment of the *Angelus;* "We are thinking of what the Saint, Simon, son of John, might say to you himself, were he here instead of his poor successor to speak to you on this his feast. What would he say to you? Perhaps St. Peter would repeat to you those words of his which, because of the present condition of the followers of Christ, we make today our own: *"Fortes in fide"*. (Be ye strong in faith!). May Mary, she who was blessed for having believed", help us to understand the lesson of Peter".[25]

Strong in faith, with the help of Mary; for this his children had prayed in their psalms and hymns and in their recitations of the Rosary; and in him, as he put down the pen, there took shape a vehement resolve to be like that: to imitate in resolution — if need be unto the shedding of his blood — the man who as Simon had been so deplorably weak.

Nunc scio vere quia misit Dominus Angelum suum et eripuit me de manu Herodis... (Now do I truly know that the Lord has sent his angel and has snatched me from the grasp of Herod). It was the *Introit* of the day, feast of St. Peter, and they were the words spoken by Peter as he went out through the Iron Gate, freed from Herod's chains. It seemed to him he could now apply them to himself, in terms of his resolve: as though the Lord (hearing those who had been unheard by him) had granted the prayers they had offered for him and for his liberation, not only during the past night, but for many a day. They were like the prayers for Peter, mentioned in the Epistle, offered by the persecuted infant Church: *"Oratio autem fiebat sine intermissione ab Ecclesia ad Deum pro eo"* Prayer, however, was offered unceasingly to God for him by the Church). — With the help and intercession of Mary; — and her hymn, fourteen centuries old, still floated in the air above where, at the first shining of the morning star, they had sung it walking in procession on the ground that was bathed by the blood of the first martyrs: *Ave, maris Stella...* (Hail thou Star of Ocean). They had sung it as though placing their prayers for him in her hands: "*Monstra te esse matrem, Sumat per te preces Qui, pro nobis natus, Tulit esse tuus*". (Show thyself a mother, Offer Him our sighs, Who for us incarnate, Did not thee despise).

It was the beginning of the eighth year of his pontificate, and he wanted to start it thus: with that *Introit* and with that same Mass, universal as was his power, as was Peter's kinglom, through which he had approached the altar of Peter for the first time — "poor", yes, but in the fullest sense "his successor". It was the same Mass with which fifty years previously "when he was young and girded himself and went where he willed", he had set out as a newly-ordained priest upon the road that was to lead him here.

He wanted to; but there were those who, now that he was old, took him and led him where they willed, and they had other ideas. They were the same people who had always made his decisions for him, without him, and against him: whom he had always obeyed and would continue to obey. It was not, however, to Peter's Cross that they were leading him. That, at least, would have given glory to God. — The prelate who had been called to receive instructions on the "liturgy of the day" had come instead to give them. They had already been established, in the "anti-triumphalistic and oecumenical" spirit of the Reform, by its executive organ for Papal ceremonies. It was to be a "community Mass in keeping with the new rite in the several languages of those composing the Assembly; the two Readings respectively in English and in French, the Gospel in Italian, the "bidding prayers" successively in French, German, English, Spanish, Portuguese, and finally in Italian..." [26]

"Why 'finally'? Why not have some Arabic or Japanese, for instance?" the Pope asked with a resigned smile. The *Cerimoniere* was in no way put out, but respectfully and ceremoniously met logîc with logic; — though later he was to be most annoyed with himself for falling into a very different kind of logic, that of the people whom in a recent article in praise of the Reform he had described as possessing "baroque eyes". Possibly because it was in Latin, he was unaware or forgetful of Seneca's famous dictum that. *"iaculum, si in solidum inciderit, in mittentem retorquetur"* (A missile, if it strikes against a solid surface, bounces back on the thrower).

"Why? Your Holiness is asking something to which he already knows the answer... there are so many different languages in the world, and there will be so many of them represented in the Assembly today, not to speak of those who will be following the service on television — that we could go on forever. If we wanted to please them all, or anyhow to displease no one, we should have to turn, or rather return, to Latin — which would be giving in to the persons who were here yesterday and all last night, the ones who were doing the praying and singing. Father Hannibal followed them around unobtrusively in lay attire, and he can tell you... it was as though the Church, liturgically speaking, was back in the times of St. Pius, and not in those of Paul VI ...happily reigning".

The sense and the adulatory tone of the last words — which in substance were a mockery — did not produce on the unhappy face of the Pope that relaxed reaction which Monsignor Bugnini's representative seemed to expect. On the contrary, his reference to the Pontiff of the Roman Missal — placed in constrast with him, Paul, the reformer — appeared to and in fact did disturb even more one in whose heart there remained stuck like a thorn the dreadful warning: *Nulli hominum liceat... Si quis autem...* (Le it be permitted to no man... If, however, anyone...).

If only he could have done so... if only it had depended on his will alone... But he could not, he had not the strenght; and in handing back the signed document, it was as though he had held out his hands again, to be led wither they willed.

"Decomposition"

All his pontificate had been like that, first resisting
and then giving in, now a protest and then a "stretching out of the hands" — as Jesus had foretold for Peter, but in a different sense, without Peter's joy,
without the glory of a martyrdom *pro Christi nomine.*
Were it but possible! If only, at the end, that were to
happen to him too! How he would welcome it.

But it was not to him they wanted to do anything.
No, through him it was the Church that they wished
to crucify — turned upside-down like Peter, not to the
glory of God but of man, turning her mind and heart
from heaven to earth and to worldly considerations.
He himself had spoken of this when he ended a long
and dolorous litany of "the heavy sufferings of the
Church" by referring to the "defection and scandal"
of ministers of the Church, "clerics and religious, by
whom today she has been crucified". He had said this
in deploring an upsurge, an outburst of "self-crit-
icism..." of "self-demolition", of "protest" against everything, which "as is logical" involves "more than anyone else, the Pope", the Church's foundation-stone.
"No one", he had said, "could have expected this after
the Council". [27]

No one, and least of all he himself, who from the
Council had expected so much. No one, and certainly

less from one person in particular than from any other. His was the protest which had pained him most; and of him, as he watched and wondered, he could in truth have repeated David's lament: "Had my enemy spoken ill of me, I could have borne it: but you! You who were but one soul with me! You who ate with me the sweet food when we went together to the house of God". — *You whom I desired to have alongside me, almost my other self, on the day of my elevation!* You to whom, for your episcopal jubilee, I sent such a letter of affection as no one before had ever received from me: "*te, quem fraterna dilectione jugiter sumus prosecuti...*"[28] (You whom We have constantly had before Us in brotherly love...).

Yes, indeed: opposition and hostility from people like Archbishop Ramsey, though he had received him with such pomp and circumstance in St. Peter's, lowering his throne in his honour, — that could always be considered as attack from "the enemy", so to speak, even though they were termed in charity "separated brethren"; but that he should be attacked by his own bishops and cardinals, and that of these Cardinal Suenens, the most privileged of them all, should be the most radical and virulent, this bewildered and pained him beyond measure. Cardinal Suenens it was who publicly, repeatedly and systematically fought against his defence of priestly celibacy and the chastity of the marriage-bed. He it was who proposed that the throne of him whom Christ had placed above his fellows should be deprived of its steps to bring him down to their same level. And the Pope had then commented. "...(This) has been said to our distressed amazement, in a manner which we consider not in keeping with the fraternal behaviour that collegiality itself demands, nor corresponding to the nature and seriousness of the problems... It is to him (the Pope), successor of Peter by will of Jesus Christ, that the right first falls of being, at the head of his brethren and in close union with them, witness to the Church's faith..." [29]

Further than this he did not go. Nothing further than his lamentations was permitted him. Even if others, dismayed by what they saw and by the gloomy picture which he himself had painted of the Church in "self-demolition", kept asking him and bègging him to bear testimony in earnest, to exercise his office also in deed. — It was forbidden him; and he would do nothing. He declared at the end of his terrifying review of the situation: "Many people expect from the Pope dramatic gestures, energetic and decisive actions. The Pope thinks there is no other line for him to follow but that of having faith in Jesus Christ, Who has a deeper concern for His Church than anybody else. It will be He Who will calm the tempest...". As though it had not been to him that Jesus had chiefly confided the government of His Church; as though he could possibly allow himself to slumber, to see and to hear nothing, whilst the tempest sundered the ship and so many were swept overboard to perish in the waves.

No; he would not take any decisive action (even though Cardinal Suenens and his associates gave him further and much more serious reason for it); he would not hear of commanding the wind and the waves, he would not say to error, or proclaim to heresy and atheism: *Peace! Be still!* He would only recommend, — nothing more. The heretics and false theologians surrounding him saw to it that he went no further.

His it was to recommend, but not to command; to feed the sheep lovingly, but collegially, and without

crook or rod; to show where the pastures were poison-
ous, but not keep the sheep away from them, nor to
isolate the infected from the healthy; to cry out but
yet not keep out the wolves; to recommend, but always
with tact, and never to command; to show zeal for the
decorum and the sanctity of the House of God, but
without scourging out the profaners and overthrowing
their tables, so as not to harm their business interests;
to recommend, but not to repress, in accordance with
the Council's didactics, — which did not apply to His
Vicar that which is said of God: *Deus qui nos et percutiendo sanas...* (O God, Who dost heal us with Thy
rod).

No, he would beat no one; he would launch no
anathemas; in his capacity as vineyard keeper he was
too soft-hearted to use the pruning-knife and revitalise
the plant which before had been a good vine but now
had become a barren bush; as a healer he shrank from
use of steel and fire, — even through he raised to be a
Doctor of the Church the woman who wrote: "Alas,
alas, the members of Christ's body are wasting away,
for there is no one left to chastise them", and who also
said that it was "the greatest cruelty" to use "ointment" where it was necessary to "cut deep with steel
and cauterise with fire".

No, he would never use such means, never steel and
fire but only ointment. Only with balsam would he
treat a patient so deeply afflicted. And the result was
such, the latest clinical diagnosis so serious, that a book
dedicated to him by a friend, one of his favourite
authors, could bear the title "The Decomposition of
Catholicism". [30].

"Despite Himself"

The decomposition, disintegration, "self-demolition" had begun from there, from the vital centre of the organism: in striking at unity in rite, language and altar, it had struck at unity in faith, dogma and morality.

Paul VI had himself asserted the vital pre-eminence of the Liturgy in the Church: *"Nam Sacra Liturgia principem locum obtinet in vita Ecclesiae"* (For the Sacred Liturgy holds leading place in the life of the Church), as also the indissoluble unity between it and the Faith itself, between the *Adoro* and the *Credo*: *"Ut autem indissolubile pateret vinculum quo fides ac pietas inter se connectuntur... Cum prorsus operteat ut lex orandi cum lege credendi concordet...* [31] (In order to show forth the unbreakable bond by which faith and devotion are linked... since what we pray must be in keeping with what we believe).

The language came first: the "providential" tongue of Rome, mysteriously pre-ordained by God to link up both in space and in time His one, universal, immutable Church: *"Lingua latina, nationum fines exsuperans..."* (The Latin tongue surmounting all national boundaries) — (Paul VI); *"Lingua latina, vinculum peridoneum quo praesens Ecclesiae aetas cum superioribus cumque futuris mirifice continetur"* (The Latin tongue, that most effective bond by which the present age of the Church is marvellously linked up with both her past and her future) — (John XXIII). The language, therefore, "of the Church", "the Church's own language", indispensable, non-expendable for the Church, as had been stated most positively by her latest Council in an injunction as clear as it was firm, which took from centuries past and launched to those to come her explicit will: *"Servetur!"* (Let it be maintained!).

This was the language, therefore, which could not but be detested and opposed century after century by the Church's enemies — by every means, through every vehicle, in every way. It was opposed now by members of the Church herself, under the specious pretexts of her own well-being and the benefit of souls; under the sophism of the harm done by "ignorance", of the linguistic "diaphragm" placed between "the assembly", the faithful, and its "president", the priest at the Altar. A new Cartesianism was born, a new religious principle: *intelligo, ergo oro* (I understand, therefore I pray). It took the place of a previous principle which said *"oro, ergo intelligo"* (I pray, therefore I understand). This was the one hitherto favoured by the Church. It meant that the ignorant — and chiefly they — were able to comprehend thanks to what is revealed to "the little ones", the humble, and denied to "the wise"; for which thing Christ offered thanks to his heavenly Father.

Until now the innovators, the ritual Jacobins, had been held in check by the Magisterium, and indeed they had but recently been condemned in most radical and forthright fashion by the most mild of Popes — *"ne contra linguam Latinam usurpandam scribant!"*

92

(let them not write against the use of the Latin tongue!). Now that he was dead, they were able to begin upon that de-Latinisation of the "Latin" or "Roman" Church, which was gradually to change the *servetur* (let it be maintained) to a *deleatur* (let it be destroyed), until, not leaving stone upon stone, they shocked and disgusted by their fury and vindictiveness persons not themselves children of the Church. Logically it was a day of much rejoicing among the groupings and sects of the Church's enemies.

Gradually, in doses, it had to be carried out, just as one administers a powerful drug; and the tactics used by the Minister for the Reform will be readily recalled. First he had people swallow in one single gulp all and more of what vernacular the Council had expressly *permitted* — "*tribui valeat*" — specifying that it was for use "*in lectionibus et admonitionibus*" (in readings and in homilies). He then called a halt, emphasising this with the logical-seeming explanation that: "the priest's personal prayers and the great "Eucharistic Prayer" (Preface and Canon) which as a prayer of consecration is *obviously* sacerdotal and not of the people, will still be said in Latin". [32] Everyone, however, will likewise remember how a very short time later, by decree of that same most eminent prelate, the Preface had now to be said in the vernacular, with the elimination thereby of one of the most stupendous examples of Christian prayer and Christian art, whether spoken or sung: and indeed not only of Christian art, but of art as such. — One thinks, for instance, of the Preface *de Sanctissima Trinitate* for Sunday Mass or of the Preface *in Missis Defunctorum*.

There was still, however, no question of touching the Canon. Of the *Regola* or Rule, as the word denotes, there would be no translation, and all the reverent solemnity expressed in its rubrics would remain intact: *"Finita Praefatione, sacerdos, stans ante medium Altaris, versus ad illud, aliquantulum elevat manus, oculisque elevatis ad Deum, et sine mora devote demissis, ac manibus iunctis et super Altare positis, profunde inclinatus incipit Canonem, secreto dicens..."* (At the end of the Preface, the priest standing at the middle of the Altar, facing it, raises his hands slightly, lifts his eyes to God, and without pause devoutly lowers them, then with hands joined and placed upon the Altar, bows deeply and begins the Canon, saying silently...). But naturally the aims and efforts of the despoilers could not stop here, on the threshold of the *Sancta Sanctorum* (Holy of Holies). In attacking the Roman Canon, thay had three goals to reach, three objectives to destroy: its Latin, its silence, and its Romanism; and they did duly attain these ends, and even more.

Blending tactics with tenacity, they started with the first and knew that the second followed logically on from it. Conscious, however, of the gravity of the step being taken, they softened it nicely by presenting what was really compulsion as mere permission: *"linguam vernaculam adhibere licet in Canone Missae"* (the vernacular *may* be used in the Canon of the Mass). They were quite certain that the bishops would see to it, no matter how they themselves might feel about it, that the *licet* for their priests would become a *debet*, the *may* become a *must*.

So it all came to pass; and though, as we have said, they did not stop there, this was a tremendous victory for the reformers — a victory against the Pope, be it said in passing, in his capacity as custodian of the Liturgical Constitution and its *"servetur"*, *"in nomine Sanctissimae Trinitatis"* (in the Name of the Most Holy

Trinity). The conquering troops were so carried away by their achievement that one of their General Staff, bishop and A.D.C. to the General himself, expressed all their uncontrollable delight in the Pope's own newspaper when he wrote the famous words: [33] "With the recitation of the Canon in Italian, the last bulwark of the celebration of Mass in Latin has now collapsed. For roughly 1500 years the great prayer has been said in Latin, and for more than 1000 years in silence". And then, as though after drawing breath and wiping the dust from his perspiring brow, he added: "The road has not been an easy or a peaceful one; it took four years!".

Four years compared with fifteen centuries; and those who were shocked by such a boast still did not and could not imagine what the unsleeping Monsignor Bugnini, principal artificer of the victory, still had in store for them — or rather for the Church. Replete but unsated, untiring, tireless, he in his turn declared: "Now that the chapter of the language has been closed, we must turn our attention to the ritual: and first of all to the Mass". It was calculated to make his followers paw the ground in anticipation, and to send a shudder through everyone else.

"We must turn our attention to..." — A sad, sadistic euphemism, which for "the Latin rites" meant the "final solution". And still the advance continued from one objective to the next towards the great, final, global objective. It proceeded to defile and destroy all that had ever existed for the sole sin of having existed. The great sin was to have formed part of a tradition that, the more it had been beloved, the more it was now to be hated. The older it was, the more worthy it was of death. It kept on with a virulence, irreverence and insolence reminiscent of Virgil's harpies over the tables of Troy — *diripiunt dapes contactuque omnia foedant immundo* — (they tear at the dishes, and befoul everything with their filthy touch) — The tables they swooped on were the Missal, the *Liber Pontificalis*, the Ritual, the Breviary, at each of which untold millions of souls had been refreshed and nourished. They were tables decked with the flowers of poesy, made gay with great songs by writers unknown or of the highest renown. They constituted that "praying in beauty" whereby a saint had once defined the function of the liturgy; whose beauty had brought so many to pray where reason alone had failed.

"Turn our attention to" signified, exactly, training one's sights on all this, destroying it all, contaminating every part of it. It was duly done, one thing after another, but this time with a fulminating speed like that of a chain of charges which demolish within seconds, or like a great flood which in a few hours befouls and sweeps away the edifice, the Cathedral, that has stood there for 1000 or 1500 years. — Everything went, from the rite by means of which we entered the Church for the first time to that through which all our forefathers — and as we ourselves had thought to do — entered it for the last. Everything, from baptism to burial; not a sacrament, nor even the smallest ceremony, was left out. With a series of Instructions that amounted to Destructions, they smashed all in sight, declaring what they did to be either accepted by or acceptable to "the people". It was reminiscent of the saying of Tacitus: *Desertum faciunt pacem appellant...* (They create a desert and call it peace...).

And what of the Pope? The Pope declared his inability to resist, his compulsion to assent. He was in the hands of those who were set on wrecking the Ritual and all connected with it. And where they went, he followed. They felt all the strength of his weakness; they were as determined as he was undecided; they counted on his tendency to yield; and they led him where they willed. The only freedom allowed him was that of expressing his unhappiness — or even at times, of seeking help to save something which under the authority of his own seal they had already condemned and exterminated.

He expressed his unhappiness to the bishops for what they had done and were doing in his name: "It happens", he said, "not without our deep anxiety and unhappiness that in matters liturgical even the Episcopal Conferences act on their own initiative and go beyond reasonable limits; — arbitrary experiments are indulged in or rites introduced which are in open conflict with the norms laid down by the Church". [34]

He looked for help when he pleaded for observance of the Council decree concerning the Church's language. Addressing himself to those urging the retention of Latin, he said: "Do your utmost to see that these words ("Latinae linguae usus in ritibus latinis servetur" — let the use of the Latin tongue be maintained in Latin rites) are faithfully put into practice, as We shall never cease to exhort you to do...". [35] These words of Pope and Council, however, would not suffice to save members of the faithful from abuse or from seeing the Pope's door slammed in their faces when they came to him on pilgrimage; when they sought permission to obey him and to continue to pray as he had said they should. As a matter of fact, when he spoke, the opponents of Latin had already, above his signature, decreed its elimination three days previously.

To deplore, to implore and then to yield. To yield by approving what in his heart he disapproved; to legalise the violation, the abuse of illegality. This was the lot of Paul VI. It was expressed once by his most immediate qualified spokesman, Cardinal Benno Gut, head of the Liturgical Department, Prefect of the Congregation for Divine Worship. To one who had manifested his bewilderment at what was happening, the tactfulness of his reply had still not succeeded in hiding the unfortunate reality: "It is our hope", he had observed, "that this malady of experimentation will cease. Until now the bishops had authorisation to permit certain experiments, but the limits of this authorisation were unhappily overstepped, and many priests, respecting no criteria but their own whim, did exactly what they pleased. These unauthorised innovations then became so widespread that it was impossible to stop them. In his great goodness and wisdom, therefore, the Pope — *despite himself* — gave in".

This statement was described as "unbelievable".[36] By virtue of it, priests and faithful now learned the origins of the "changes" and "reforms" into which their obedience had constrained them when they went weeping unto the altar of that God Who hitherto had given joy to their perennial youth. They now knew that it was not due to the will — no matter how fallible in this — of the Head of the Church. It had all been brought about by the whims and distortions of this or that petty little Luther, most assuredly also an opponent of priestly celibacy: some priest or friar perhaps already paying court to his own particular Catherine, lay or religious, and sure of his Bishop's approval, if not actually of his blessing, at the end of the road.

Profanations

Among the "innovations" thought up without authorisation, and applied without respect — or rather
with complete disrespect — for the will of the Pope, we
may take the example of self-administered Communion in the hand, another product of the Dutch factory
turning out the Protestant brand of Catholicism.

Perturbed by its abusive spread in the Church, and
informed of the intention on the part of the reformers
to have its illicit character transformed into licit, with
the practice made law for all, Cardinal Gut went to the
Person who had the power and the duty to say no. He
had, in fact, already said no in what was the most
inspired yet of his pronouncements, the encyclical *Mysterium Fidei.* It was in this that he had proclaimed:
"the method of receiving Holy Communion must be
preserved unaltered, as laid down by the laws presently
in force". He had recalled that any permission to the
contrary "to receive Communion into one's own hands"
had been granted "in olden times" through force of
necessity, during the persecutions of the Christians,
"*persecutionum violentia vexatos*" (Harassed, as they
were, by the violence of persecution), and "*absente
sacerdote aut diacono*" (in the absence of priest or
deacon). He had added that those first Christians were
so imbued with reverence for the Sacred Species that

"they considered themselves guilty of misdemeanour, and rightly so, as Origen records, if for want of attention they allowed some fragment (of the Host) to fall".

Armed with this, and with the whole of Christian tradition behind him, Cardinal Benno Gut went to the Pope and begged him not to give his consent to this further surrender to Protestantism. Already we had Communion standing up, the practice by which they had expressed their denial of any divine presence in the Host and their consequent refusal to offer worship. — He had actually gone on his knees before the Pope, saying he would not get up until he had the assurance that consent would not be granted. The Pope did, in fact, give this assurance, and Cardinal Gut went off happily. However, Monsignor Bugnini alerted Cardinal Suenens on the matter. Cardinal Suenens immediately swung into action, and he in his turn paid a visit to the Pope too. The Pope passed the question on to the bishops. And the bishops, by the over-whelming majority of 1215 replied with a negative *non placet*. The Pope, then, pointing out amongst other things that "the manner of distributing Holy Communion has behind it a tradition going back for many centuries", that "it expresses the respect of the faithful for the Eucharist" and that "it serves more efficaciously to avoid any danger of profanation", thus concluded: "Wherefore the Holy See earnestly exhorts bishops, priests, and faithful to observe the existing law, only recently confirmed by the Catholic Episcopate, for the common good of the Church. [37] But then, very shortly afterwards, in the Pope's newspaper, there appeared the following from a certain bishop: "So far as concerns the method of receiving Communion, complete freedom is left to the faithful. You may receive it as you have done hitherto, on the tongue, or else in your hands... *no one can impose upon you or forbid you either one rite or the other*".[38]

No one. - And what, then, of the Pope? The Pope again gave in. Yet once more he let things take their course. Self-administered Communion spread, and amongst its various effects one saw the Host being placed in the tremulous hand of the aged or in the irresponsible hand of childhood, to risk falling to the ground and being trampled by those pressing forward in the queue behind. This was also to be the way with the "wine" (for we do not dare say the "Blood"), with drops being spilled on the ground during the "dipping" or "chalice" or "spoon" Communion which Monsignor Bugnini had himself introduced, this time with explicit and binding reference to the Protestant method which he indicated as a model and used to impose a veto. When the Common Cup was presented by a "suitable minister", either a priest "or a young theological student" the communicants were forbidden to pass it from one to the other. This was stated to be "a method alien to the Liturgy, *even in the "supper" of our separated brethren*", but anyhow, this method involving drinking from the same vessel happened less frequently. In part it was probably due to the immoderate fervour of those whose turn came first. At times, despite appeals to see that enough was left for the others, or to consecrate several chalices, the vessel would unhappily be left empty too soon. In part there was also the finicky disposition of certain people who would rather go without this kind of Communion or "supper" than indulge in it. It happened sometimes even with the "dipping" method, because there would be "ministers" whose accuracy was affected either by excess or inadequacy of years, and they would dip their fingers too into the chalice or vessel, as would appear from their wiping them afterwards on their handkerchief or on their clothing.

There was a fourth Communion rite which was little practised, not because it was less fitting, but because it was still less agreeable. It had been invented by the reformers, or rather they had adopted it, for it was already commonly used for purposes of public hygiene in establishments which sold Coca-Cola and similar beverages; and it was also used among friends in South America for the drinking of 'maté': Communion "by suction", or "with drinking-straw", it was called in the official text of the new *Mass Rite* "promulgated by Paul VI", in the "Standard Edition for Italian Liturgy", approved *perlibenter* (most heartily) by the Congregation for Divine Worship and published by the Italian Episcopal Conference (with all rights reserved, copyright by Italian Pastoral Publications). The procedure was described as follows:

"Communion by drinking-straw is carried out in this manner: the principal celebrant takes the drinking-straw, saying: *May the Blood of Christ keep me unto eternal life,* drinks the Blood of the Lord, and immediately purifies it by sucking up a little water through it from a vessel previously placed on the altar, then putting it on a paten provided for that purpose. Near the chalice, there must therefore also be a vessel with water for the purification of the drinking-straws, and a paten on which these are to be laid. The concelebrants, one after the other, approach the altar, take a drinking straw, and drink the Blood of the Lord; they then purify the straws by sucking a little water up through them, and lay them on the paten provided...” — After the concelebrants' Communion there follows that of the faithful: *Communion rite under both Species with drinking-straw*: The principal celebrant too uses ses the drinking straw for receiving the Blood of the Lord... After this, whoever is to receive Communion stands in front of the deacon who says: *The Blood of Christ.* The communicant replies: *Amen,* and with the drinking-straw which the deacon offers him, he drinks from the chalice the Lord's Blood. Then, being careful not to let any drops fall, he sucks through the straw a little water from the vessel which the deacon is holding in his hand. He then places the drinking-straw in another receptacle. If there is no deacon present, the celebrant himself offers the chalice to each Communicant and an assistant alongside him holds the vessel containing the water to purify the straw. — It will be among the tasks of the new-type sacristan, therefore, to prepare “the drinking-straws for the celebrant and for all those receiving Communion by drinking-straw”, as well as “a vessel containing water to purify the drinking-straws and a paten on which these will be laid...” — There is no mention of what is then to be done with the water, but it is implied that it will not be consumed, even if together with the saliva or lipstick from so many mouths there must of necessity be some trace of those drops of what we shall term and wish still to consider as *wine* — being filled with repugnance at the thought of having to read “drinking-straw” alongside the “Blood of Christ”.

The edict which contained the above, along with all other novelties of the “New Mass”, bore the signature of Pope Paul VI; and if we refer to this fact again, it is not thereby to assert that Pope Paul VI approved of

"Communion by drinking-straw" but to demonstrate what horrors he has been made to legalise, "despite himself", by innovators of whom it would be charity to assume that their inventions were the product of diseased minds.

Luther's Revenge

We had a famous example of "oecumenism", "pluralism", and other -isms which are the legitimate off-spring of Modernism, in a species of interdenomination-al festival which took place in the Papal Basilica of St. Paul's Outside the Walls as previously arranged, and as duly described later, by the *Osservatore Romano.* [40] Those present sang in different languages simultaneous-ly. The opening chorus of the Ritual specifically got out for the occasion began as follows:

"Peuples, criez de joie et bondissez d'allégresse!
Praise to the Lord, the Almighty, the King of creation!
Lohe den Herren, den machtingen König der Ehren!
Pueblos, cantad con alegria, saltad de gozo!"

We have to admit that however little edification may have resulted, at least there was any amount of "*allegresse*" and "*gozo*" in the great cathedral. Some people were reminded of Babel, and others of a game called "musical misunderstanding", an old game, a pop-ular pastime in the hostelries, which consisted of singing different songs at once. Others, again, even among some of our "separated brethren" present in the role of sightseers, were more disgusted than amus-ed, and pondered upon the destiny of the Apostle who, there of all places, right over his tomb in Rome, was

105

to see translated into reality what he had indicated to the Corinthians as an absurd hypothesis: "If we were to speak the various languages simultaneously in church, and some outsider or unbeliever were to enter, would he not perhaps say: but have you all gone mad? — *Nonne dicent quod insanitis?* —".

This took place in Rome, at the centre of the Catholic Church, under Catholic auspices; and the only language not to be admitted to that multi-lingual pantheistic rite, even with the possible title of the *unknown god*, was Latin. — A god unknown indeed, deliberately ignored and shut out, save for three conventional little words signifying that the rite was all in order, duly approved now and for the future by the relevant authority. For the Ritual, produced by the Vatican presses, had printed on its back: *Cum permissu Superiorum.*

Nonne dicent quod insanitis? And say it they did, those separated brethren, now separated more than ever, as they turned and retraced their steps. They said it to the Pope himself on questions of language, doctrine, and indeed all else. He made reference to it — though with small effect on those who in his name had given their "Superiors' permission" — when he warned Catholics: "The greatest danger for oecumenism lies in Catholics becoming enthusiastic about what Protestants have already discarded as harmful, and forsaking on the other hand all those things of which Protestants are now discovering the great importance". Another of their number informed a Vatican prelate that "also and above all as a Protestant theologian" he was "extremely worried about what was happening in the Catholic Church".

More than worry it was the anguish of the son

106

who had gone astray. In the midst of all the hunger and misery in which he found himself, he had taken comfort from the tought that the lovely, well-appointed house of his father, which so rashly he had left, was at any rate still there awaiting his return. Now, in contrast with the parable, his comforting dreams were shattered; and as he drew near, in all his anticipation, he saw that the house was being demolished ("self-demolition" it had been termed). Despite all the father's tears and supplications, it was now being torn down by the son who had stayed at home. And he turned sorrowfully away, not knowing where else he could go.

Yet another of them, one of the best-known, René Barjavel, had asked with equal concern what was happening to the Catholic Church, when he wrote as follows in 1969: "The Church is moving... the celebrant who for two thousand years had turned his eyes to the altar, that is to God, now has turned his back upon it to look towards the faithful, This makes me think of a ship whose pilot, standing in the bows, instead of looking at the sea and the stars, turns towards the passengers to join in their conversation. Where will the ship end up? I, a Protestant, have the dim feeling that this Protestantisation of the Catholic Church will be harbinger of I know not what disasters". [41]

"*Où ira le navir...?*" The pilot of Peter's barque was asking himself the same question. As he flew on this other ship towards the shores of Turkey, he was more than ever aware of it, and more than ever oppressed. For, as the sheets of the "Mao Mass" that he held in his hands now confirmed, Protestantisation had reached the very heart of the Church, the Mass itself.

His depression kept on growing. During the flight news had reached him that Monsignor Edward Walsh was dying in the United States. This was the venerable bishop, victim of the man on whom he was about to call, to whom he had said as he embraced him at Castelgandolfo on his return from Mao's Chinese prison: "The Pope thanks you in the name of Christ for all that you have done and suffered." And as he had done in the case of Padre Pio, the stigmatist, he had granted him the favour begged of him, that of being allowed to say the same Mass as he had said before his imprisonment, the only Mass he had ever celebrated.

The greatest shock Bishop Walsh had received on leaving his Shangai prison was to find that with all the desire and hunger he had upon him, after twelve years fast from it, the Mass was now no longer the same either in language or in rite. This had been the worst of all his sufferings; and still almost incredulous, he had asked the Pope with simple candour "Why?" — The question put to him then, as it had been put before and after by so many others, had never yet been answered. And now it came back to him, with the memory of those two eyes that had gazed at him with a pitiless innocence resembling that of a child, and asked "Why?".

Why?... Why?... Why?... He comforted himself again by recalling what his cardinal friend had said to him jestingly to restore his peace of mind. "Scruples", he observed to himself, repeating his friend's words; and taking up again the pages of the "Mao Mass" he set himself determinedly to study them. Determinedly, like one who has taken a firm decision and is resolved not to go back upon it. — But it was only a breathing-space, and his decision this time was disturbed, strangely and mysteriously enough, by a poet, by the greatest of poets, the undisputed monarch of his far-off classical studies.

The *Ma-Ma* had come down lower to get beneath the clouds which had formed over the Aegean after Lepanto, and heading for the Dardanelles and Istanbul, it was now flying over Anatolia. Its tourist guide and commentator drew attention to a village on the deserted plain below not far distant from the sea, and vouchsafed the information that there, bearing then too the same name of *Ilion* as today, but better known as Troy, there had risen once the city sung by Homer. "The river, the trickle of water which you see", he said, "is the Scamander...", and suddenly, strangely and misteriously, just as he was steeling himself in his new determination, the Pope remembered these relevant, particular lines:

Ἀλλ' ὅτε δὴ τὸ τέταρτον ἐπὶ κρουνοὺς ἀφίκοντο
Καὶ τότε δὴ χρύσεια πατὴρ...

(But both of them being come for the fourth time to the Scamandrian waters, the great Father raised the golden scales in the heavens... and the fatal day of the Trojan leader dropped towards the Bear. Sorrowfully then did Phoebus forsake him.)

Strangely and mysteriously; for these lines had lain buried in the depths of his memory all down the years since his distant schooldays. Their sudden emergence seemed to him bound to hold some special sign for him and he stirred uncomfortably.

Only a short time previously he had stirred just like that for something of as little importance as Card-

109

inal Bugnini's accidentally knocking over the statute of Our Lady with his arm, and now he thought of it again, In itself it was nothing; but not for him, for he had not forgotten how the same thing had happened at his table in the Vatican, with the same person involved, on that sad Maundy Thursday of April 3, 1969, when he had signed the death-warrant of the Roman Missal.

It was naturally an accident then too; a jerky movement due to the haste with which in his excitement and impatience Monsignor Bugnini had handed him the pen with one hand and pointed with the other to the foot of the document as he said: "Here." An accident, wholly understandable in the legitimate exaltation of a winner breasting the tape; but yet that falling down of the statue, as though Our Lady had wished to avoid the sorrow of seeing what was happening, had thoroughly upset him. It was as though he had been looking, not at her statue but at her, the Mother of Jesus, at the moment when Pilate was signing the sentence and giving the order of execution: *I, lictor: expedi crucem!* (Go, lictor: prepare the cross!).

Because it was in the Missal now proscribed that Jesus had continued to live on. It was by virtue of it that He had remained upon earth, Man and God, as he had once been in her womb. Through it He had been uninterruptedly reborn in untold millions of Hosts, in countless millions of raised chalices, uninterruptedly present in the Tabernacles of the world; — whilst in the new missal, that of the "new epoch", only the *memory* of Him was destined to live, in virtue of a *supper*, also called a Mass, *sive Missae*, consisting in a "gathering of people, presided over by a priest, for the purpose of celebrating the memorial of the Lord": *ad memoriale Domini celebrandum.* This was exactly according to the definition of Luther when he rejected the "abominable Canon by which the Mass is made a sacrifice", and insisted and explained that "The Mass is not a sacrifice... Call it benediction, eucharist, the Lord's table, the Lord's supper, memory of the Lord, or whatever you like, just so long as you do not dirty it with the name of sacrifice or of action". [42]

This, the substance, had been the goal aimed at, more or less openly, right from the beginning, — even if without the excesses which an excommunicated Luther had levelled against the Mass he had abandoned: "I affirm that all brothels, murderers, robberies, crimes, adulteries are less wicked than this abomination of the Popish Mass"; and without his predictions or delirious expectations of what would happen after its so deeply longed-for overthrow: "When the Mass has been overthrown, I think we shall have overthrown the Papacy. I think it is on the Mass as on a rock that the Papacy wholly rests... everything will of necessity collapse when their sacrilegious and abominable Mass collapses...". [43]

As to the method for reaching this conclusion, Luther himself had already demonstrated just how much notice was to be taken of objections, in so-called free discussion, or of any negative decisions arrived at. Exactly similar, so far, had been the line of action followed by the "executors" of a "Liturgical Constitution", fashioned, one would say, to be made mock of and trampled upon. The method was still precisely that. — The "New Mass", Monsignor Bugnini's Mass, had been democratically rejected by the majority of bishops in the 1967 Synod; but it was then brought by him to the Pope, so that he might use his authority to impose it, and to condemn the former one as being guilty, apparently, of first of all not being Monsignor

111

Bugnini's, and then also of being and declaring itself to be "Roman". And yet once more authority gave its voice to arbitrary demand, and imposed and condemned.

This, the decisive victory over the reluctance of the judge, marked the end of an unjust trial, the last act of a passion in which the Church had first been despoiled of her raiment, the "seamless robe" of "her own language"; then scourged, disfigured, mutilated; buffetted and derided; and all of it had been permitted as part of the judge's vain efforts not to reach the final sentence.

He had been urged even by "pagan" voices to save her — *Nihil tibi et illae!* (Let there be nought between thee and her), but he only repeated, more and more convinced, but equally more and more weak, *Quid mali fecit? Ego nullam invenio in ea causam...* (What evil has she done? I find no fault in her...); till at last, surrendering to his weakness, declaring or having it declared on his behalf that he had yielded despite himself, he pronounced: "I am innocent of this thing: do ye therefore what ye will".

He insisted, and this was not denied him, that in the introduction to the sentence of death on the Missal there should be written what is given below. It was an introduction which constitued a plea for acquittal. It honoured the Missal with the highest praise, letting not the slightest shadow fall upon the recognition and exaltation of its merits. It said: "The Roman Missal, promulgated in 1570 by our predecessor St. Pius V by order of the Council of Trent, was welcomed by all as one of the many admirable fruits which that holy Council distributed throughout the whole Church. For four centuries, indeed, not only has it supplied priests of the

Latin rite with the pattern for the celebration of the Eucharistic sacrifice, but it has been spread through almost the entire world by the saintly preachers of the Gospel. Furthermore, innumerable saints have abundantly nourished their devotion towards God through its readings of the Holy Scripture or through its prayers; and the general arrangement of these goes back in great part to Gregory the Great...".

In order to display less obvious absurdity in passing from eulogy to condemnation, — or, in other words, from what the judge had done of his own volition to what the judge had had forced upon him, — the reformers did not shrink from using false testimony. They cited witnesses on their behalf people who had spoken out clearly, strongly and repeatedly in the opposite sense. One was horrified to find among such, at the very outset, someone like Pius XII, the Pope of *Mediator Dei,* who had branded as unhealthy, pernicious modernism re-emerging from the cesspool of "Pistoia Conference" all and each of the reforms spawned after Vatican II and now flourishing together in the *Novus Ordo.* Here, in fact, is what Pius XII had to say; "The rash and presumptuous behaviour of those who deliberately introduce new liturgical practices is to be severely condemned". And this is taking place, he says, "not without great unhappiness" and "in things not just of small but of very grave importance". In the leading position among the rash he puts "whoever uses" (or would like to use) "the vernacular in the celebration of the Eucharistic sacrifice". He reminds them, or rather informs them, precisely in that Allocution to which a note in the new edict invites reference, that "it would be superfluous to point out that the Church has serious motives for firmly preserving in the Latin rite the unconditional obligation on the part of the celebrating priest to use the Latin language". "Serious motives", "firmly", "unconditional obligation": each word is a hammer-blow by which the Church emphasises "yet once more" that law which divine Providence, the authority of her Popes and Councils, the wisdom and virtue of her doctors, the devotion of "innumerable saints", and the experience of centuries have handed down to her and enjoined upon her to preserve, as in *Servetur!* (Let it be maintained!).

In order to achieve their ends of eliminating the Mass and the Missal in favour of a "New Order" which no one had thought of or asked for, which everyone found to be beyond imagination or belief, the reformers had forgotten, ignored or anyhow violated a fundamental paragraph, one of the *Normae Generales,* in the Liturgical Statute: "There must be no innovations in the ritual where this is not made necessary by some real and certain advantage to the Church"; and whether or not this was to be considered an innovation, and what kind of innovation it was, we were to hear from the Pope himself. Only a few days before sentence was carried out, he — the judge — in a series of rhetorical questions and exclamatory phrases, informed us, seeking vainly to convince both us and himself of its inevitability, — "The change has something surprising, something extraordinary in it, for the Mass has been considered the traditional and unalterable expression of our religious worship, of the authenticity of our faith... Why, then, such a change?... Why such an extraordinary novelty?" He would show most marked dismay on the very eve of execution, as he saw before his eyes the extremely negative reply to the other questions of whether the change, the *innovation,* was *useful* or *necessary* because of some *real and certain advantage* conferred thereby upon the Church. He was to repeat, but now with all the bitterness of regret, what he had stated, as though asking for pardon, in the introduction to the sentence: "New Mass rite! It is a change which affects a venerable, centuries-old tradition, and thus touches that religious heritage of ours which seemed as though it was to enjoy an immutability beyond any interference, and to put on our lips the prayers of our forebears and of our saints, to give to us a strength deriving from loyalty to our spiritual past, — a past to be made our own and then passed on to future generations. At a moment like this we understand better what is meant by historical tradition and the Communion of Saints... it is a change which will have its effect upon the faithful... and we shall find that it is the saintly who will be most perturbed by it... The priests themselves... It is no small thing, this novelty..." [44]

The "New Mass"

The priests more than anyone else; for it was they who had to say this "new Mass", and no longer just THE MASS. They envied the faithful because, in their common misfortune, they at least had the luck only to have to assist at it, only to see and hear it. It was the priests, too, who had to instruct their congregations and lead them to look upon it as something good, as the real good, in contrast with all they had ever so far taught.

Erravimus (We were mistaken) they had now to say. (And if there were those who could not bring themselves to say it in words, they had to imply it by their actions.) We, your teachers, your pastors, they said, hitherto and right from the start, have mistaught and misled you; we, the Church, the Popes, the Councils, the Saints, have all of us until now, possibly in good faith or through our ignorance, if you like, been completely mistaken: the Mass, it turns out, the real, authentic, valid Mass, was not the one of which we told you that there were saints who went into ecstasy in the saying of it. No, it is this one, this new one which, just to take its name, is no longer to be called a Mass, but a supper ("a supper, or a Mass"), so that you should, using the appropriate, corresponding phrase, no longer talk of *going to Mass but of going to supper...*

Erravimus indeed; we had all of us got every single thing wrong from start to finish.

Beginning afresh, giving logical explanations, they would eventually teach that the altar was no longer to be called "altar" or to be considered as such: it was a "table" ("*altare, seu mensa*" — altar or table); and that one tablecloth, only one, would be sufficient, just like at home or in any restaurant, instead of the three symbolic altar-cloths, This would be laid, too, as was much more fitting, by women. There would clearly be no consecrated stone, no relics, and if it had not been put away already, no Tabernacle. Instead of the Host, there would be a loaf "a loaf of large dimensions", which the head of the table, the "priest-president", would share between himself and the other diners.

All would naturally be on the same footing, all comrades. This would be made plain straightway by that broken off bit of the *Confiteor* where almost all of those asked to intercede for us found themselves suppressed. It was to be said in chorus, with no one taking it upon himself to give absolution after it "*in nomine* and *in persona Christi*". — The absolution would, in fact, be abolished. And if sin was not to be abolished with it, any sense of it would afterwards be greatly diminished when the triple protest of unworthiness to receive Christ became only one and that collective. Most consistently, Christ would no longer be received in a kneeling position, as we have already pointed out, but standing up. On the other hand, any thanksgiving there was would be indulged in henceforth when seated.

It was as leading comrade, then, that a priest would preside over the supper: a vivacious, garrulous supper it was intended to be, with women skipping around as

118

helpers extraordinary between door and table: *"Mulier-ibus licet... fideles ad portas ecclesiae recipere eosque in locis ipsis convenientibus disponere"* (Women may... receive the faithful at the doors of the church and conduct them to their places). Women, too, on exactly the same footing as men, would act as readers. — A lively supper, in raiment "unbecoming for Electra"; for black would be outlawed from the liturgical hues even for the mourning of Good Friday. — This, we might point out, explicity contradicted what Pius XII had laid down when he listed among unacceptable novelties, deviations from the straight path (*"ex recto itinere"*), requests for the exclusion of black from the liturgical vestments (*"Liturgicas vestes nigro carere colore"*).

It would be a truly democratic supper — in shirt-sleeves, so to speak — with vestments already thinned out and, whilst still calling for alb and stole, tending to disappear altogether. The chalice would no longer be of noble workmanship or "gilded within" — as once was prescribed and now is forbidden. It was to resemble the common drinking-glass, and already it was being suggested that it be actually made of glass. A cordial supper between friends it was to be, with no more spikenard being wasted on the principal Guest. All the marks of veneration, adoration and love, of which the Mass was full, had to go. No more altar-kissings. Henceforth these things would be for the other guests: there would be kisses, handshakes, embraces, pats on the shoulder, and anything else implying that the more we were together, the happier we should be. — A social supper, for the workers, where work would duly be a topic of conversation. The terms used would be those of a tenant-farmer talking to his landlord: not any longer a miserable little hired labourer, but a very evolved cultivator of the soil. The bread is product of the earth and of our enterprise. And if the wine is called fruit of the vine, one knows that the vine's roots are sunk in the soil, just like those of the wheat, and need our help to fructify. — A "community" supper, a "people's" supper, with no "mysteries", no chanting, no musical instruments unless they be popular ones — a festival-supper: to put it in one word, a Lutheran supper. And if Lutherans, in recognising this, in some cases rejoiced and in others deplored the fact, Catholics could have nothing but tears for it.

Priests there were who prayed God, as they sadly recited their *Introibo* for what time they might, that He would take them to Himself before the arrival of that day, the stipulated 30th of November. Others asked themselves whether after all they had not been mistaken in thinking they had a vocation. They asked the question with all the grief of betrayed love, in an excess of bitterness which only proved how irresistible had been their call, and how joyous their response to it. Of them indeed it had been true that their *Introibo*, both in its anticipation and its reality, had given joy to their unending youth. One of them wrote of the others, expressing the thoughts of all: [45] "that Holy Mass which they had longed for ardently from their seminary years, which for tens of years they had celebrated, and which constituted the greatest and most indescribable consolation, the substantial nourishment of their priestly lives...". He too went on to ask the reason for something which could not possibly have right or reason, and continued: "It has been the joy, sole comfort and daily bread of us priests who tread the ways of the world without belonging to it. Only God himself knows how many sufferings, temptations and

120

inner sorrows have vanished as we pronounced the sublime words at the altar and carried out the hallowed rites, drawing upon the treasures of that Holy Mass which now they wish to take away from us." "This is our drama", he said, and trembled in the saying of it. "We became priests to celebrate that divinely sublime Holy Mass; in it we were conscious of what Cardinal Schuster called 'the heart-beat of a thousand generations of martyrs, doctors and saints'. Perhaps — and my heart trembles in saying this dreadful thing — could we have even remotely foreseen (what was going to happen) our hands today would not be consecrated...".

On the numbers and type of priests who were experiencing this drama, Cardinal Ottaviani and Cardinal Bacci had already spoken to the Pope, with all the authority attaching to their names: "Among the best members of the clergy this takes the form of a nerve-racking crisis of conscience. We have countless examples of it every day"; and what they said of the clergy, they repeated of the laity in the famous letter wherein they had attempted to obtain a stay of execution. Their petition logically caused a certain anxiety among those who, by the excessive pressure of their *crucifige*, had wrested the verdict from the judge's weakness. They now found allies in Sinedrium and Lodge in the vilification of these two stout defenders. The *high priests* had joined with all the Church's enemies, of whatever category or hue.

The two cardinals pointed out that the *Novus Ordo* represented "both in its entirety and in its details an amazing departure from the theology of the Holy Mass", an "extremely grave break" with what the Church at Trent had definitively laid down with the intention of erecting "an insurmountable barrier against any heresy attacking the integrity of the Mystery". Well aware as they were of the bewilderment which the announcement alone had produced among the faithful, they wrote: "All the new elements introduced into the *Novus Ordo Missae,* and in contrast with this the lesser or changed place allotted to what is perennial — if indeed there is found for it any place at all — could turn into certainty the doubt already unfortunately creeping into many minds: that truths which have always been held by Christian people can be altered or suppressed without disloyalty to that sacred deposit of doctrine to which the Catholic faith is eternally bound. The recent reforms have adequately illustrated that new alterations in the liturgy can only lead to the complete confusion of the faithful, who are already showing signs of restiveness and unmistakable diminishment in their faith...".

These were grave words, but they were to be confirmed and outstripped by the facts, for lessening of faith often became complete loss of it; and the churches, the Church, was abandoned by many simple people, little fitted to grapple with the new, diverse, adverse, perverse "theology". In their eyes, the changes, the new, the latest "liturgy" had rendered her altogether unrecognisable. "The New Order"? "The New Mass"? For them the adjective was at odds with its substantive. They had known a Mass without any qualification, and its unchangingness had been for them like that of the sun; always the same, never old and never new; never less bright or less beloved in their eyes and hearts. It was like the seasons for them, always coming round again, always bringing flowers and fruits as good and as beautiful as ever.

The facts, as we have indicated, rapidly began to

outstrip anything that had been foreseen; and deform-
ation took the place of reformation, so that the children of the original Reform, with whom and because
of whom the new reformers had forsaken their heritage,
now began to denounce all that was objectionable in
it and wanted no part of it.

Non est species ei neque decor... (There is neither
beauty nor majesty in it...) And how much the more
must it have seemed so to those who had loved their
Mass no less for its beauty than for its sanctity.

The Mass is Ended

No: they, the Catholics, the simple Catholic faithful, who knew nothing of the intrigues which had produced it, did not and could not recognize their Mass, *The Mass*, in that *quid simile* or poor imitation of divine service, that Lutheran by-product evolved by people with no claim to Luther's literary talents, and indeed so far removed from them that their decrees and texts offended grammar and syntax as much as their doctrine offended orthodoxy.

Sive Missa (or Mass) they had defined their product, and never did conjunction serve so well to signify disjunction. The "New Mass" was in complete contrast with all that they, the simple faithful, had until now known and loved; that had seemed "destined to enjoy an immutability beyond any interference" like the sun, like the seasons. It was without any *Introibo* this "New Mass", — what Mauriac had described [46] as "that ninety-second psalm which rose up like a wondrous portal at the entrance to every Mass"; it had no *Confiteor* save that shred of one which left out Our Lady, the angels, apostles, saints, the whole heavenly court before whom it was recited; it lacked the prayer at the foot of the "holy mount", along the path of the "tabernacles".

There was no supplication of the Most High in that symbolic triple trinity of ejaculations. The nine times which also recalled the chorus of angels, was reduced to "two or more" as the celebrant pleased. There was no longer any *Gloria* unless in exceptional circumstances; and we had readings from a Bible-serial which had absolutely nothing to do with the Mass. These were often rendered, too, by ladies not always adequately covered either from the head down or from the knee up. The Apostle who had commanded "*mulieres in ecclesiis taceant*" (let women be silent in church) and who had forbidden "*mulierem non velatam orare*" (any woman with head uncovered to pray — i. e., to participate in divine service) might never have spoken. — There was no proper Offertory, no *Lavabo*, no tinkling bell. There were only a few seconds between the *Sanctus* and the Consecration, with the Consecration being spoken like all the rest in a loud voice, "in ordinary reading tone", into a microphone. Knees were given the least trouble possible, and the least possible reverence was offered to Him Who was now held in the priest's hands. Nor was there the extreme care that once there was not to lose any particle, despite awareness *tantum esse sub fragmento quantum...* (that Christ was as much present in the tiniest fragment as in the whole). — Despite the memory of a certain woman who thought it too much to touch even the hem of His garment.

This process of divesting the sacred of its sacredness, the deliberate matter-of-factness used in handling, eating, and giving to eat just like any ordinary piece of bread Him whom, as the 'Imitation' warns us, "*reverentur angeli et archangeli, metuunt sancti et iusti*" (Angels and Archangels worship, the holy and the just hold in fear), — all this made the "New Mass" a very different thing indeed. It made it very difficult for the simple faithful to recognize their own Mass in it or in its liturgical novelties — among them, as we remember, "Communion by drinking-straw".

Great then, loud and universal, was the cry of grief which went up now from Catholics not already stultified or drugged by the preceding gradual reforms. Widespread and urgent was the appeal made to the Pope — in the wake of that which had already come from the two cardinals. It came from other cardinals bishops, heads of religious orders, priests, and lay people of every country and every walk of life. He was urged to rectify by its annulment what through his weakness, "despite himself", he had brought about by his approval. *Errare humanum est* (to err is human) and Peter too, as a man, had erred. And no man is lowered by it to the same extent that he is elevated by admitting it. It matters not how humble be the prompting; it need only be, for instance, the crowing of a cock.

The fact that Paschal II, despite himself, by reason of his weakness and whilst under duress, signed a decree like the Bull of Investitures does not overshadow his memory as much as his words of condemnation spoken to the Lateran Council illumine it: "What I did, I did as a man", he said, "because I am but dust and ashes; wherefore I do confess to having erred, and I beseech you to pray God to forgive me. That accursed document I hereby do condemn with perpetual anathema, so that its memory may be held in odium through all centuries to come, and I exhort you all to do likewise." The Fathers, as we know, duly did so, calling out in unison: "Fiat! Fiat!". [47]

The Pope was, in fact, reminded at the time of this precedent in an effort to induce him to reverse his sentence. It must certainly have given him much food for thought, especially since his own case had not the extenuating circumstances present in that of his predecessor. Unlike him, Paul VI was not a prisoner in the hands of someone like Henry V. He could not plead in human justification that he had been constrained to act "in order to free the Church, the people of God, from a host of evils". If he had been put *in vinculis... in animam inimicorum eius* (into chains... into the power of his enemies), this had been something depending completely on himself; and so far as concerned the Church and the people, he well knew that no one whatever had asked for what had become a grievous source of disturbance to all.

All appeals, however, all supplications, all arguments were to no avail. To the noble letter from the two cardinals he had replied indirectly in one of his Wednesday talks, exalting in lyrical terms the importance, holiness and beauty of "ecclesiastical tradition", but adding for their benefit: "The Church is like a musical concert: not even a leading instrument can afford to play in an orchestra as and how it likes". [48] A splendid metaphor, a most telling one, except that in this particular instance it would have been more apt, more in keeping with the reality of things, to speak not of a concert and of an orchestra, but of a small-time dance-band with whose electric guitars it would certainly not do to mingle the solemn tones of the organ.

All too well he knew; but if his was the baton used, his was not the arm that conducted the orchestra. The bishops, in their turn, were tools of a minority, who were in turn tools of an oligarchy; and this in its turn was the tool of Monsignor Bugnini. The bishops rejected a final attempt to obtain postponement of what, "despite himself", he had sanctioned. And so, on November 30th, 1969, there came into effect "the new epoch of the Church": on that day, with the advent of the "New Mass", one could truly say: "*The Mass is ended*".

. . . .

On that day Paul VI hesitated before appearing at the usual window, and those who saw him close up noted that his face showed signs of a deeper suffering than ever before. It happened that he had read again in the course of the night those stern words which *all* his predecessors from then on had followed, respected, and feared as something sacred and never to be violated. He felt now a horrible sense of foreboding at being the first, the only one ever to have dared challenge them: "*Huic Missali nihil unquam addendum, detrahendum, aut immutandum hac Nostra perpetuo valitura Constitutione statuimus et ordinamus... Nulli ergo hominum liceat...*" (That nothing be ever added to, taken away from, or changed in this Missal, we hereby establish and command by this our Constitution which is to be valid forever... Let it therefore be permitted to no man...).

Could he yet... He almost dared hope there were still time... He inquired about this and that... He wanted to know everything, everything that was going on; he was curious, for instance, about what was printed on the black-bordered leaflets that the late autumn wind was tossing about with the leaves from the plane-trees down there below. They said, in point of fact, just this: "On this day, November 30th, 1969, the new reformers have decreed the death of the Holy Mass as it has been celebrated for centuries throughout the entire earth! From Rome, centre of Christianity, there arises a cry of indignation and of protest. As the waters of Egypt were changed to blood, those of the Eternal City have now been turned red...". He asked to see the newspapers at once, and in all of them, along with news of the fact itself and of the protest made, he read comments on lines more or less similar to the one taken from one of the most moderate of them: "The die is cast. Something which never happened in the course of long centuries has now been accomplished by the decree launching the new *Ordo Missae*, effective as of today. This means that the spiritual world of Christian, Catholic, Roman, Apostolic man has been practically suppressed, and has been replaced by another type of Christianity very near to that of the Protestant sects. Millions of Catholics are asking themselves why the Pope (has done this)". [49]

The "total confusion of the faithful" which the two cardinals had foreseen was now a fact; and even Monsignor Bugnini in the Pope's own newspaper grudgingly had to admit this. On the following day one of his lieutenants had written on his behalf: "It was not unforeseen that the dissentient voices we had heard might represent a state of mind shared by large groups of the faithful. There were members of the faithful who yesterday did not attend Mass..." [50]

Such were the first fruits of the exercise; and as it had been in Rome, so it was elsewhere, and in much greater measure than the delegated observers referred back or than those who had done the delegation dared to confess; this desertion of the churches, for many people meant abandonment of the Church herself. She had been guilty in their eyes of betraying the loyal trust they had placed in her. *Ego quidem te... Et tu facta es mihi nimis amara!* (I made you my finest vineyard, but you became for me exceeding bitter!).

And the Pope, what of the Pope? He tried very hard to believe on behalf of "the millions of faithful"

130

who were asking themselves why, what it was desired he should believe by the few who ran the show. — Such had been the beginning? Its reception even by "large strata of the faithful" had been called negative and hostile? What of it? The fruits were not yet ripe; it was too soon to judge; and without referring directly to what can be done for fruit with time and a little straw, the same pen quoted above wrote in the same newspaper: "How often a reform that eventually has proved itself providential has had to strive hard to establish itself at the outset!" — He forgot, poor man, that with the "New Mass" they were turning their backs on Trent; and that the Book today being dispatched for pulping had for its title precisely "*Missale Romanum ex decreto Sacrosancti Concilii Tridentini restitutum*" (The Roman Missal restored by decree of the Most Holy Council of Trent). It was at Trent they had spoken of the "difficulties" being encountered by their decrees — and it was naturally from the Protestant innovators and their sympathisers that the difficulties of those days had come. And he wound up with a large dose of ingenuousness by saying: "Yet the good worked by that Council over a period of four centuries is today generally recognized throughout the Church".

Just a little patience, then, he said. Stand fast against all recrimination, reason, logic, fond memories and regrets. Everything which today provokes resistance, for reasons of mind or heart, tomorrow will come to be accepted by sheer force of habit. As he put it: — "Who will help them to understand their error? Perhaps time, the settling of the new rite into the habits of the faithful..." But is not this process of getting used to it and settling in what makes the bird happy in its cage, where once it beat its wings against the

bars and would touch no food? And the good Monsign-
or need not have read Machiavelli's *The Prince* to
be aware that force of habit will tame peoples who,
at the beginning, saw their young men ready to go
through fire for freedom.

Patience, therefore, was the motto; but not too
much. And Monsignor Bugnini himself wanted to push
on. He was bringing down his baton before the score
was ready or the parts distributed; and it was the
Pope who asked just as the curtain was about to go
up: "But how can we celebrate this new rite if we
do not yet possess a complete new missal, and when
there are still so many uncertainties about its application?"

Monsignor Bugnini had unwillingly granted "to elderly and infirm priests the faculty of continuing to say
the Tridentine Mass" — but only for a short time and
as something to be hidden, *sine populo* (without any
congregation), as though it was something to be asham-
ed of. Something, one might say, that should have
made millions of priests, bishops, and Popes blush during four hundred years. He had also warned the bishops not to be over-generous with these dispensations:
they had to be sure that only "really exceptional 'cases'
would be able to take advantage of them." [51] And the
bishops in general were docile in this too: they showed
understanding with priests who were modernist, free-
thinking, Communist, matrimonially-minded, in favour
of divorce, with homosexual tendencies, detractors of
Our Lady, anti-dogmatists, and what have you; but
they were strictly on the look-out, keenly alert, that no
one in their dioceses, young or old, healthy or ailing,
should attempt to say such a thing as *that Mass*.

Patience then: give time a chance. But time was

falling down on the job. It was too slow in fulfilling the thinly-veiled hope that hall the dispensees would eliminate the nuisance they represented by setting off for Paradise with their baggage of Latin and Gregorian Chant. So Monsignor Bugnini came back with another *diktat*. His new missal had finally made its appearance. In contrast with the four hundred year old stability of the other, it had been, as a consequence of the "uncertainties" referred to, altered no less than four times in about as many months. Anyhow, it was now proclaimed that "it *MUST* gradually eliminate the old ritual of the Mass permitted, as a concession to elderly priests, up to Advent 1971". [52]

It was not thus, though he had every reason for doing so, that the great, the saintly Pius V had behaved with the Roman Missal. And that he had every valid reason for doing so is sufficiently clear from the opening lines of the introduction to that *Quo primum tempore* which was posted on the portals of the Basilica of the Prince of the Apostles (*"ad valvas Basilicae Principis Apostolorum"*) on July 29, 1570, and intended to have universally binding force for all time: *"Cum unum in Ecclesia Dei psallendi modum, unum Missae celebrandae ritum esse maxime deceat, necesse iam videbatur..."* (since it is eminently desirable that in the Church of God there should be one way of chanting and one rite for the celebration of Mass, it was now seen to be necessary...). The objective was to bring back Catholic worship from the pluralism and dispersal of divided churches to the unity of the Church herself.

It was a pluralism, anarchy, and disorder precisely like those which the *Novus Ordo* under the guidance of the Vincentian Monsignor Bugnini is tending today to re-establish. — It would be useless, we suppose, to counsel him to read what his holy founder, the good "Monsieur Vincent" had to say to his first sons as he impressed upon them "uniformity in action": [53] "What shall I say of the Church's feelings in this matter? Does she not practise uniformity in her rites? Is not what is performed in Rome performed also in France, in Germany, in Poland, in the Indies and everywhere else? Has she not perhaps the same sacrifice, the same sacraments, the same ceremonies, *the same language wherever she be?*" And after pointing out in what concerned uniformity of language "the drawbacks there would have been if each country had had the Holy Mass in its own language", he continued: "It has been, then, her desire that all her sons should be unanimous and uniform in everything... Why? Because, apart from the fact that this universal practice is in itself an honour to God, this same conformity ensures the avoidance of a number of serious abuses". He recalled the pluralism and anarchy that there had been in the past: "Oh, if you had seen, I do not merely say the unsightliness but the diversity in the ceremonies of the Mass, you would have blushed for it: there is nothing in the world more ugly than were those different manners of celebrating Mass".

He had witnessed, he said, "eight priests saying their Masses each differently from the others: a variety to make one weep" — (though at least they were all still saying them in Latin!). This, however, was nothing compared to what would now be witnessed through the handiwork of one his own sons. Differences in the manner of celebrating between nation and nation, diocese and diocese, between one town and the next, one church and another, one altar and another in the same church, and between priest and priest using the same altar. The altar itself would be built or rebuilt to face in two directions, so as to accomodate those wishing to celebrate facing the people and those desirous of doing so facing the Tabernacle. It was not just pluralism but unbridled license, anarchy. The good Monsieur Vincent would have covered his eyes and quietly wept could be have foreseen that a son of his would go so far in his introduction of variety to the liturgy as to arrive at Communion by drinking-straw. "Praise be to God", he had exclaimed, "that it has pleased His divine goodness to remedy such disorder!" and the remedy, that divine remedy, had been just exactly the Missal, the *Missale Romanum* — which was not something dreamed up, the work of "innovators", but *restitutum*, restored *"ad pristinam sanctorum Patrum normam ac ritum"* (to the original pattern and rite of the saintly early Fathers), to be used *"in quacumque orbis parte"* (in all parts of the world) *"perpetuo"* (forever), *"ad ecclesiasticum purum retinendum cultum"* (to preserve the integrity of ecclesiastical worship) essential to the unity of the Church.

Unity in integrity. This was the *"unum sint in veritate"* (let them be one in truth), it was the *"unam sanctam"* (one, holy) that had to be defended and maintained against the great heresy which proclaimed the opposing principle, *cuius regio illius et religio* (to every region its own religion, its own form of worship) a heresy which rightly regarded the Mass as the rock on which the Church rested.

A situation such as this might surely have justified refusal to make exceptions or issue any dispensation from conformity to the law, But this was not how the saintly wisdom and magnanimity of the legislator visualised things. We read with astonishment in the solemn *Quo primum* quoted above that exemptions are indeed allowed from the rule, not for a period of one or two years, but permanently, and not extended for reason of age or health to a few, but collectively. All those belonging to branches of the Church which possessed a liturgy already approved by the Holy See "and having an unbroken history of more than two hundred years" were told they could retain it: "...*amplectantur omnes et observent... nisi ab ipsa prima institutione a Sede Apostolica approbata, vel consuetudine, quae, vel ipsa institutio super ducentos annos Missarum celebrandarum in eisdem Ecclesiis assidue observata sit*". Not only that: they were not merely permitted but urged to remain loyal to their centuries-old tradition, "*praefatam celebrandi constitutionem vel consuetudinem nequaquam auferimus*" (the aforesaid practice or custom of celebration we have no intention of abolishing). Furthermore, even if they preferred the Missal now promulgated, they actually had to receive dispensation from the Bishop, or appropriate Prelate or Chapter, to use it, after which the Pope too would dispense them; so that they were *allowed to conform* to the new rule rather than to take advantage of any exception: "...*sic si Missale hoc, quod nunc in lucem edi curavimus, iisdem magis placeret... iuxta illud Missas celebrare possint permittimus*" (thus, should they prefer this Missal which we have now promulgated... We *permit* them to celebrate Mass in accordance with it).

"We permit them". In observing both the wisdom and the humanity of this disposition, we may properly gauge the brutality and lack of wisdom contained in the MUST of this latter-day legislator who compels the aged and infirm to leave the scene at the end of a two-year period should they wish to remain loyal to a law "valid forever", which is to say, still effective,

with its unbroken, universal four hundred years of effective tradition behind it.

Because the law, no matter what, remains what it
was intended to be: irrevocable, undeformable, un-
changeable — by anyone whatsoever; and its sanction
remains that of the wrath of God, — not just threatened, but foretold, plainly predicted. Let him who dared
make the attempt clearly realise that he incurred the
wrath of God. There were no doubts about it. And the
fact that out of his weakness he had displayed such
temerity was, for the Pope, from that 30th of November onwards, a perpetual source of dread.

That day too he had said his *Angelus,* and then also
it had seemed to him that Our Lady had looked at him,
not in the happiness of the Annunciation, but in the
grief of the Mother whose Son they had crucified.

From Deep to Deep

How many times since then had she appeared so to look upon him, further afflicting his tormented soul.

For, as time passed, and as Catholics, both priests and faithful, did not so much absorb the "New Mass" and its side-effects as fall beneath its deadening influence, so more and more did his soul feel the tightening grip of the sanction he had defied, a terror of that arm which seemed forever pointed at him from beyond the Roman tomb. "*Si quis autem...!*"

Time had indeed been given, and still God continued to grant him more. In seeming contradiction of the phrase *Non videbis annos Petri* (You will not see the years allotted to Peter), he busily carried forward his long Pontificate. Not only had he been given time: he had been preserved from many perils, like the dagger at Manila in far-off unhappy 1970. This too was something he would never forget. But had not all this been given him for a purpose? Was it not the mercy and patience of God giving him the chance to make amends? *Dedit ei Deus locum poenitentiae, et ipse...* (God gave him time for repentance, and he...). But for how much longer would it last? This was something he would ask himself with apprehension as each anniversary of his election brought the reminder that with his *Accepto* he had not only received upon his brow the most august of earthly crowns, but on his shoulders the weightiest cross of human responsibility which he could neither share nor pass to others. *Iudicium durissimum his qui praesunt* (Hard will be the judgment on those who rule) — And in him, Cephas, the Church's rock, weakness could be forgiven very much less than in anyone else.

Weak, however, he was, as they all knew; for well had they used this *to lead him where he did not will to go* — to lead him from the ill-fated 7th of March to the horrible 30th of November; and now, being afraid of the very weapon they had exploited, the reformers found ways of deceiving him and of concealing from him the consequences of the greatest of all his liturgical surrenders. They did all they could to make him forget everything connected with the Mass, and kept before him only their own "New Mass".

Thus it was, too, when a great centenary came round, the fourth centenary of the Roman Missal. This was a date which the Church under any other Pope, whether a Pius XII or a John XXIII, would have celebrated with encyclicals, pastoral letters, congresses, and pilgrimages to Rome from all over the world. It was, instead, passed over in silence, totally ignored. On that day, July 11, 1970, the *Osservatore Romano* did not condescend to give it even a single line — just as it had shown a similar forgetfulness, we may add, for certain modern Papal edicts — like Pope Paul's own *Sacrificium Laudis* declaring the Church's language and music were to be considered indispensable to the Mass and never to be given up.

Another centenary, however, one of a different kind, was not allowed to go unnoticed by the Church's representatives. We refer to that of the breaching of

140

the walls of Rome in 1870. Adopting the proposal made by the well-known Father Balducci that the event should be marked by a "day of penance", that is to say of expiation for the Church's sin in waiting for the troops of Savoy to make their "opening", as it were, (with all that this might mean) — flowers were gathered in the Vatican Gardens and sent "for those who had fallen at Porta Pia"; whilst at Porta Pia itself the Cardinal Vicar celebrated "this day of destiny" with a Mass, a parade, and a speech of such Garibaldian content that there were people who thought it overdone and suggested some small thought might have been given, perhaps, "to those who had fallen on the other side": to those, in other words, who had given their lives for the Pope.

During those same days, and in the same spirit of appeasement, availability and peace, the Church in Italy had let its own walls be breached, but in much more deadly fashion, The divorce law was conceded to the Church's enemies by those in Parliament and government who were supposed to be her friends. They were worried only about the indissolubility of a political matrimony which would keep them in their jobs, and they enjoyed the support of not a few ecclesiastics who saw in acceptance of the law a potential bargaining counter, or a guarantee against trouble. Trouble in this case was the "religious war" threatened by the Marxist-Masonic hard-liners and feared at all levels by a clergy in whose ranks the Wolseys moved by fear or self-interest again outweighed the Thomas Mores.

A very sad year indeed was 1970. Whilst in Rome the Pope's gardeners twined wreaths and garlands for Porta Pia, and the "Catholic Party" ran up the white flag on the battlements of Christian marriage, in Brussels the Pontiff's closest friend, Cardinal Suenens — almost his *alter ego* and forecast as his successor — was busily plaiting for him a bitter, hostile crown of thorns. Like the *Bersaglieri* bearing down on the Eternal City, he launched his attacks in an inter-Christian or rather inter-heretical "Theological Congress" presided over by the heretic Schillebeeck. The Congress closed with demands such as these: "that the Pope, the bishops and the clergy be elected by all members of the Church; that women too be admitted to the priestly ministry and to the diaconate (episcopacy and Papacy likewise understood);" "that Pope and bishops listen carefully to the theologians before taking decisions; that the *Creed* be reformulated and adapted to the mentality of modern man; that the basic structure of the Church be radically reformed; that the Church participate more directly in public life; that full freedom of inquiry and expression be finally conferred on all students of the science of God and in general upon all the faithful". The new *Creed*, a truly oecumenical one, was to ignore all distinction between Catholic and non-Catholic, embracing and recognizing only "Christians": "Christians" of every denomination and sect, brought together by means which the Cardinal, aspiring to Luther King's phrase "I have a dream", saw as yet only in his own dreams. "I do not know how the decisive encounter can be reached. Will it be a Vatican III? Perhaps. But since in dreams it is possible to overcome all obstacles, why might the final *rendez-vous* not constitute a re-launching of Christianity, and why might the Council of reconciliation not be a second Council of Jerusalem?" [54]

The Pope once more bowed his head; and the bishops had never a word to say on his behalf. They failed to dissociate themselves from their colleague.

They were much too busy seeing there were no priests saying a Latin Mass.

But why talk of dissociation? In one way or another the Suenens-Schillebeeck demands were all given due consideration, and already we saw a first result of this in the matter of Papal election, when Paul VI himself, with a *motu proprio*, proclaimed the reform, *Ingravescentem aetatem*. This was less a reform than a revolution: a full-scale *coup d'etat*. By means of it, in either a casual or a cynical flouting of a Constitutional Act like *Vacante Sede Apostolica* and of the Code of Canon Law, the wisest members, by age and experience, of those entitled to the normal dual right contained in any civilised legislation — the right to elect and be elected without any upper age limit — were now deprived of it. Those cardinals who had reached 80 years of age were now automatically deprived of their vote and excluded from Conclave (*"ius amittunt Romanum Pontificem eligendi atque in Conclave ingrediendi"*). The world looked on amazed as it witnessed the Church thus spurning the divine precept: *"Honora personam senis"* (Honour the person of the aged); and there were those who remembered what the Latin author had said of Rome: *"Ingravescente iuvenum insolentia ruit Respublica"* (The Republic is perishing through the growing insolence of youth).

Lex orandi lex credendi (What we rightly pray we rightly believe)... Just so. And the reformation or reformulation of the *Creed* in the name of the "freedom of inquiry for all the faithful" was the consequence, yet another one, of the reformation of prayer in the name of the "right of all the faithful to understand". It was a reformation which, beginning with form, had on that 30th of November reached substance as it

143

substituted the "New Mass" for the old insuperable barrier by which the Church had said to heresy of every kind and sort: *Hic confringes tumentes fluctus tuos* (Here will your foaming breakers spend their force). The barrier progressively weakened had finally collapsed; and now the waves of heresy — of every kind and sort — were spreading their filthy flood over all the Church's sweet meadows, sweeping away, destroying, befouling and blighting *omnia quae in eis* (everything therein).

It was in those days of melancholy 1970 that one read reports like the one published by the French press of a church in the Isère loaned by its parish-priest and so re-arranged "with removal of the altar and candlesticks as to provide room for a regulation 'ring' and permit the staging of an international boxing contest".[55] It was then too, in the days of the Suenens-Schillebeeck "Theological Congress" to reformulate the Creed, that the lay press carried the following report culled from the Catholic news services of Belgium and other countries: "Among the items of information coming in from Brussels, where a 'progressive' theological congress is taking place at the moment, where problems of sex are being authoritatively discussed, one in particular has made an extremely strong impact on Roman ecclesiastical circles. In a certain church in the Belgian capital, the symbol of virility was raised over an altar in a licentious setting of youthful dancers. The church in question, according to the Catholic sources narrating the episode, is a Capuchin one "transformed for the occasion into a hippy temple". At the entrance to this church dedicated to St. Francis, "young people in white robes writhed and twisted, waving cords and chains, and everyone was offered bread and wine, cigarettes and grapes". The reaction of some of the more extreme elements, it seems, had prevented the liturgist of the word there present "the celebrated American theologian Harvey Cox" from speaking, and there had been "a great deal of shouting and yelling until the culminating moment when, as a Catholic agency states textually, from behind the altar there rose up an enormous phallus in transparent plastic". [56] The newspaper added that Cardinal Suenens himself, the Archbishop of Brussels, "could not refrain" from protesting. But there was no excommunication forthcoming, no interdict upon the church, either from him or from Rome; nor indeed did any condemnation whatsoever appear anywhere, possibly out of respect either for the "freedom" referred to previously or for that "liturgical pluralism" which is blood-brother to all the other "pluralisms" that would turn the Spouse of Christ into the harlot spoken of by the prophet.

The barrier was now down, and beyond yawned the deep. From whirlpool to whirlpool, from deep to deep it beckoned, down into darkness ever more profound to where beneath it all leered the Prince of Darkness. Paul VI now saw happening before his eyes, but in absolutely unforeseeable measure, what he had once warned against and deplored when, in 1966, the Reform was at its beginnings and the first cracks in the defensive seawall had begun to appear. These were the cracks which had fully justified the alarm sounded by a certain writer; and though the Pope at that time had found himself "constrained", [57] *despite himself,* to speak against him, he had nonetheless been unable to hide his anxiety over "certain episodes of rebelliousness", or to avoid lamenting a current tendency which made him wonder whether the liturgy, or what the innovat-

145

ors termed such, could still lay claim to the name, or whether any religion reduced to this level could still call itself Christian: "...*propensio quaedam eo tendens ut Liturgia, si hoc nomine adhuc appellari potest... et una cum ea, quod necessarie consequitur, ipsa christiana religio*".

This tendency, this "new mentality" he had insisted, "whose sinister origins it would not be difficult to trace, on which it is sought to base the demolition of authentic Catholic worship, implies such doctrinal, disciplinary and pastoral subversions that We do not hesitate to consider it as an aberration. We say it in sorrow, not only because of the anti-canonical, radical spirit which it gratuitously professes, but by reason of the religious disintegration which it inevitably brings in its train". This was the clarity of vision, the prophetic utterance of one who in his day had laid emphasis on the classical dictum of *"Principiis obsta"* (Stop the beginnings); and the phallic festival, the Brussels "liturgy" (in that unhappy 1970) was only one instance amongst all those which showed how right he had been.

Because of the intimate connection between the pattern of prayer and that of belief, which the Pope had repeatedly affirmed, what was happening to the ritual was being reflected in every other sector. In keeping with the Suenens-Schillebeeck request for popular appointment of the Pope — as well as of bishops and priests — which was now well on the way to actuation, he had a request from the International Theological Commission, which he had founded and filled with his own favourite representatives. They said that out of deference to the "separated brethren" and to "episcopal collegiality" he should drop such titles as

146

"Head of the Church" and "Vicar of Christ". And this he did in effect do, though not formally renouncing the prerogatives, by no longer using them in his Allocutions and Decrees, just as he no longer wore the tiara during ceremonies. *"Filios enutrivi et exaltavi, ipsi autem spreverunt me..."* (My children I nourished and raised up, but they did spurn me).

Not least of his sorrows in this context, not the least humbling of his humiliations, was to have to disown, to treat as though they were not his, those sons of his who truly were, those who loved him as much and as earnestly as it seemed he did not love them: who had never endeavoured to strip him of his titles or rob him of his office; but who kept imploring him to exercise it, to be Pope in deed as well as in name, to be truly Head of the Church and Vicar of Christ. He knew very well that, though they suffered because of it, they did not love him any the less for having received from him, on that distant day in 1970, a stone instead of bread, a scorpion for an egg, and a serpent for their fish. It was the occasion which the radio had now recalled, and which he himself could never forget.

But yet, notwithstanding everything, the keys to his heart, so to speak, the faculty to bind and loose on his behalf, still remained in the hands of the others, of those who sought to remove from him the keys of Peter. They were people who were capable, as was illustrated by the heading of the *Nuovo Osservatore Romano*, of inter-twining them with the hammer and sickle, — symbols of work, it is true, but emblems also of the Party which Lenin had described [58] as "implacably hostile to religion" and of an ideology which Pope Paul had termed "the negation of Christianity".

Yes, notwithstanding everything: notwithstanding all the ill-use made of those keys to his heart, all the "subversions" perpetrated through the binding and loosing that the others did in his name, — for by now they had reached key positions and controlled the levers in every sector of the "Ecclesiastical Community" which once had been called, and used in fact to be, the Church; notwithstanding the persecution inflicted by them on "the rebels" as they defined them — on those, in other words, whose Creed was still the Creed of old, whose Mass was still the real Mass, and whose supreme guiding principle was to obey God rather than men.

There were still a number of such people around, among both priests and faithful, even though they were driven into the "catacombs" by the edicts of bishops who were now all "new", all "young", at least in ideas if not in years. The law obliging those over 75 years to retire had naturally done its work, and those "old" in ideas, even though they might be younger in dynamism than the men who replaced them, had now been got rid of. — We repeat that there were still some around, — but not for long; the decree ensuring their final elimination was drawn up and ready inside Cardinal Bugnini's brief-case; it only awaited the signature, at the opportune moment, of one who shortly before had shown a certain weakness in the matter of the Mao Mass.

Excommunication

The occasion, the opportune moment, came quite unexpectedly as they flew over the North of India. The plane was due to land at New Delhi before the last leg of the journey into Mao's empire, and there had been a radio conversation with the Archbishop concerning the Mass which the Pope was to celebrate in the new cathedral.

"Which Mass?"

While protesting his own personal submission to whatever His Holiness's decision might be, the Archbishop did not hide the fact that the opposition of the Indian Catholics to the New Order, which had now lasted for almost ten years, was still inflexible.

"Still" was the operative word, for the Cardinal Prefect of the Department for Divine Worship was only too well aware of their initial rebellion, based on their loyalty to the Roman tradition. The *Osservatore Romano* at the time had made this acid comment upon it: [59] "In our day it happens sometimes that even the most opportune measures, bearing the authentic seal of authority, are made the object of criticism. This is the case now in India. Widespread opposition has led the Indian bishops to make a complete re-appraisal of the entire question, keeping in mind both the criticisms themselves and the motives which gave rise to them...".
The seriousness and widespread nature of these critic-

149

isms, as well as the determined nature of the opposition, had caused Monsignor Bugnini himself, at the bishops' request, to grant India a special *vacatio legis;* but this dispensation had expired some time ago, and the fact that the "rebellion" still continued, that priests and bishops were still saying Mass as if the 30th of November 1969 had never happened, and that the Indian primate should put this question to him now, simply filled him with rage:

"You ask me which Mass? In that case, none at all!" and quite sure of his ability to handle the Pope, he then informed the pilot that unless there were technical or other reasons for it, the stop at New Delhi could now be considered cancelled.

The Pope had just handed over the text of the message he was sending to Mao, since they were fast approaching the Chinese territory of Tibet, when Cardinal Bugnini, still seething with anger, asked to be received and came into the compartment.

Holding in his hand the document he wanted signed, he launched out on an attack upon the "rebels". Beginning with the conversation he had just had with the Archbishop, and enumerating all the other grave examples he could call to mind, he demonstrated that the Reform, the whole Reform, was now in danger, and that along with it went the Council, the *aggiornamento* of the Church, oecumenism and, in fact, his entire work as Pope. The achievements which would see him pass into history as Paul the Innovator would be all of them undone unless it was at once decided, he said, "to take a very strong line, and cut down, root out by excommunication, what we have not been able to bend or to train with time and with patience". "Yes, by excommunication", he repeated emphatically, as he saw the Pope wince at the word, — "by the very weapon which they reproach us for having thrown on the scrap-heap. The moment has come! We had... Your Holiness had allowed a stay of two years; for India here we had most reasonably stretched it out; and now, after almost 10 years, we have this bishop asking us: "Which Mass?" This is just the very moment!" And thus saying, he held out the document.

It was a document hatched and lengthily prepared in Rome; and along with it he held out the pen which he had kept in memory of April 3rd, 1969. The Pope on that day had given it to him after signing *Missale Romanum*, the death sentence of the Roman Missal, and the birth-certificate of his own New Mass, the Mass which the Catholics of India had refused to recognise or accept in its lack of true Roman tradition. — With this pen already in his hand, and the ink wet upon it, the Pope still hesitated over signing. Then, making an effort to avoid ratifying this persecution warrant, made out and dated in the language of Rome *"Pridie Idus Iulii"*, he said:

"...*Sub poena excommunicationis!*" But isn't that too strong? Won't there be danger that..."

Cardinal Bugnini understood at once and, without letting him finish the question, he replied:

"Danger? *Utinam ut abscindantur qui vos conturbant!*" (Would that those could be removed who upset you).

At this, the Pope placed his hand on the sheet and doubtfully, tremulously, his eyes seeking vainly for those of Our Lady, he wrote: "Paulus Pp VI".

High in the sky, which had suddenly gone livid and dark, there came a roll of thunder, and in it the Pope thought he heard a voice, as it were, which said to him:

151

"Paule, Paule, quid me persequeris?" (Paul, Paul, why persecutest thou Me?)

So it seemed to him, but naturally it was not so (for no one else heard it). None the less, his Damascus was at hand; and after a second, louder peal, yet another one, very loud indeed, announced this to him, precisely at the moment the *Ma-Ma* flew into the Chinese sky above Tibet.

The First Mass

He found there waiting for him the numerous escort of planes which Mao had sent to meet him, and the noise of all those engines did not drown that of the march — *The East is Red* — with which they greeted him, flying above, underneath, and around him. Inside, the hostess was handing him, together with the telegram of reply, a bouquet of red and white carnations from the President, when that third and loudest peal of thunder shattered the sky; and this time it was accompanied by a fork of lightning which seemed to the Pope to take the shape of an arm pointing straight towards him: That arm!

Struck by the lightning, the aircraft gave a shudder and a lurch, but then straightened out again, whilst the plane's escort swept off like frightened birds. A moment later, however, the same voice which had been inviting everybody to remain calm, suddenly called out in alarm:

"Parachutes! Put on your parachutes and jump: we are losing height..."

From the ripped tank a stream of fuel was pouring out, and the winged monster had only a few minutes left before it would fall bloodless to the ground.

In the chaos which followed — barely held in check by the voice which kept repeating the instructions to be followed — somebody yelled out in desperation that

153

his parachute had jammed, and the others saw and heard the Pope, who had left his compartment, smilingly give him his own and help him to adjust it.

He had put on his papal attire and, looking every inch a Pope, he blessed them all gravely, majestically, serenely. The hostess, struck by the gesture, and not panic-stricken as were the others by the impending disaster, offered him hers. But going back into his compartment and kneeling with the little statue of Our Lady in his hands, he replied with the same smile:
"No: I shall remain, *since God grants me this grace,* I must remain. Go now, you must jump before it is too late..." As she once more insisted, he smiled again and said: "Go, and don't have any fear for me: I too have my... parachute..." Kissing, then, the beloved image, never more beloved than now, he prayed as she, the hostess, had told him she had been wont to do: "*Monstra te esse matrem: Iter para tutum...*" (Show thyself a mother: Make safe my path), except that, thinking of the path for which he now prayed, he raised his eyes and added "*Ut videntes Jesum, Semper collaetemur...*" (That looking upon Jesus, We may forever rejoice).

He remained there, kneeling in prayer, whilst the aeroplane, pilotless and out of control, continued in its descent like a bird wounded and dying, and whilst the others, swinging from their parachutes, dangled in the air shivering with cold and fear.

. . . .

None were lost, as he had begged that it might be, and from all sides they converged on the spot where the plane had fallen: the Pope was alive.

He was alive, lying prostrate on the earth, but no one dared approach him, for they heard him speak, and yet neither understood nor saw with whom... It was a strange, mysterious dialogue between earth and heaven, of which they caught only two questions:

"*Quis es, Domine?*" (Who art thou, Lord?), and trembling at the reply:

"*Domine, quid me vis facere?*" (Lord, what wilt Thou that I do?). He was fatally injured, though it was not visible, and he arose with difficulty. As he did so, like a man coming out from a vision, his face was as pale as the snow on which the aircraft had crashed after its long fall... Yes, they were all there, including the crew of the *Ma-Ma*, with the hostess too; and she, with a woman's solicitude, tried to protect him from the cold by placing round his shoulders his clerical cloak that had been taken from the wreckage. After offering thanks to the Lord, he held out his arms for support and said:

"Let us go".

In the words and action he was obeying the voice that he seemed again to hear, saying to him: "*Surge et ingredere civitatem et ibi dicetur tibi quid te oporteat facere*" (Arise and go into the city and there it will be told you what you must do); and sure enough, there close at hand, was a "city". It was a village of wretched huts huddled round one a little less wretched than the others, and over this one there was a cross which, mounted on a tiny belfry, revealed it to be a church. A church indeed it was, a Catholic church, a small, courageous outpost of the Faith in Mao's vast empire. It was served by missionaries who had stayed on with their Tibetan faithful in this lost corner of the Roof of the World to cultivate that Faith through the sacraments, and to bear witness to it with their blood on the day that the agents of atheistic activism should discover them.

155

The Pope's journey there was a painful one. The bewildered missionary who welcomed him asked: "*Sacerdos es tu?*" (Are you a priest?). He never for a moment imagined that most of the others, dressed as they were in lay European attire, were priests too, or indeed bishops and cardinals.

The Pope answered: "*Utique, frater: sacerdos romanus sum*" (Yes, my brother: I am a Roman priest), and without further revealing his identity, he asked whether he could say Mass.

At the sound of the bell, the parishioners came hurrying eagerly to church from their houses, their looms, their animals; and great was their wonder at sight of all these strangers, some of them gathered outside and smoking, some seated or standing inside the wooden walls. But their wonder was no more marked than was the devotion and reverence they showed as they entered and knelt down to pray in what was for them the House of God — the dwelling, therefore, that they had desired to be and had made the most beautiful and ornate, the richest, or anyhow the least poor, of all their poor huts.

Despite the gravity of his injuries, when the Pope had finished a long prayer of preparation and was about to celebrate, his face was shining with a joy that none had ever seen there, except perhaps when, as a young man full of energy and zeal, in his native parish of Concesio in Brescia, he had ascended the altar as a priest for the first time. Before vesting (though now, since "preparation" had been abolished, they were excluded from the Missal) he had recited the same psalms as he had said then, beginning with that same antiphon — never before said with more faith and compunction: "*Ne reminiscaris, Domine, delicta nos-*

tra... neque vindictam sumas de peccatis nostris...
Quam dilecta tabernacula tua, Domine virtutum! Con-
cupiscit et deficit anima mea in atria Domini... Inclina,
Domine, aurem tuam et exaudi me, quoniam inops et
pauper sum ego... Quia misericordia tua magna est
super me, et eruisti animam meam ex inferno infer-
iori..." (Remember not, O Lord, our misdeeds... Nor be
revenged upon our sins... How lovely are Thy tents,
O Lord of Virtues! My spirit longs and faints within
the courts of the Lord... Give ear to me, O Lord, and
hear me, for I am poor and needy... For Thy great
mercy is over me and Thou hast snatched my soul from
the depths of hell).

With the same devoutness as then, he had put on
the sacred vestments which the new rites had discarded, kissing them and saying the appropriate prayers;
and his lips had lingered long on the maniple which
the missionary held out to him, the cross joyfully
embraced, as he murmured the invocation: *"Merear*
Domine, portare manipulum fletus et doloris, ut cum
exultatione recipiam mercedem laboris..." (May I be
worthy, O Lord, to wear the maniple of tears and suffering, that in exaltation I may receive the reward of my
labours). The moment had come: the moment of tears
and of rejoicing for what been lost in Rome, in St.
Peter's, and found again here, in this Tibetan hut,
among these Christians, both priests and faithful, to
whom persecution had given the great good fortune
not to have known that other wilderness. And thus,
with tears of mingled grief and happiness, repentance
and new-found understanding, the Mass began.

It began as it did that day at Concesio, and all the
space of years between, all the present diversity of
circumstances, people and things, did not prevent him
from seeing himself once more among his family and

friends. He heard their voices, and in them there seemed to be echoes of voices innumerable from every age and clime; they were merged in one, as their hearts were joined in a single beat, and their minds in a single act of faith, when he made the Sign of the Cross and said: *"In Nomine Patris et Filii et Spiritus Sancti, Amen. Introibo ad altare Dei"* (In the name of the Father and of the Son and of the Holy Ghost. Amen. I shall go unto the altar of God); and the response came from those Tibetans, men and women, old and young:

"Ad Deum qui laetificat iuventutem meam". (To God who giveth joy to my youth).

He overcame the emotion which caught at his throat and continued:

"Iudica me, Deus, et discerne causam meam de gente non sancta: ab homine iniquo et doloso erue me" (Judge me, O God, and distinguish my cause from those who are not holy; deliver me from unjust and deceitful men); and they in their turn readily and serenely replied:

"Quia tu es, Deus, fortitudo mea: quare me repulisti? et quare tristis incedo, dum affligit me inimicus?" (Because Thou, O Lord, art my strength: Why hast Thou cast me off, and why do I go sorrowful, whilst the enemy afflicteth me?).

The hostess, perhaps re-living her days in the Scottish hostel, joined them in the responses with a fervour that seemed as deep as their own; whilst the others, cardinals, bishops, and priests, apart altogether from any disdain they professed for Latin, had by now forgotten it all through lack of practice and took no part in them. Cardinal Bugnini stood looking mutely on.

Mute and stricken, he watched and listened as the Pope, with these inhabitants of the Tibetan mountains,

recited the psalms of David, just as if for him and for
them the fateful 30th of November had never taken
place.

"*Emitte lucem tuam et veritatem tuam: ipsa me
deduxerunt et adduxerunt in montem sanctum tuum
et in tabernacula tua*" (Send forth Thy light and Thy
truth: they have led me and brought me unto Thy
holy mount and unto Thy tabernacles).

"*Et introibo ad altare Dei: ad Deum qui laetificat
iuventutem meam*" (And I shall go unto the altar of
God: to God who giveth joy to my youth).

"*Confitebor tibi in cithara, Deus, Deus meus...*"
(To Thee, O God, my God, I shall give praise upon
the harp...).

The Pope did not leave out one single rubric; he
remembered them all. Cardinal Bugnini continued to
watch. Now it was *altari se profunde inclinans, iunctis
manibus* (bowing deeply towards the altar, with hands
joined...). He heard him say the old *Confiteor*, naming
one by one all those Saints who had been dismissed;
he saw him, helped by the missionary, ascend "the
mount" in pain and joy, praying in a low voice, as was
now no longer permitted; he saw him kiss the altar with
the first of that series of kisses which had been abolished, a long and loving kiss as though of reparation
and of reconciliation; he saw that this dual spirit now
seemed to permeate every word and action of the Mass.

Exercising a power which the missionary was still
far from suspecting him to possess, he had decided to
say the Mass for May 5th, and it was with a humility
as deep as his devotion that he read the prayer: "*Deus,
qui ad conterendos Ecclesiae tuae hostes, et ad divinum
cultum reparandum, beatum Pium Pontificem Maxi-
mum eligere dignatus es, fac nos ipsius defendi praesi-
diis, et ita tuis inhaerere obsequiis, ut omnium hostium*

superatis insidiis, perpetua pace laetemur..." (O God who, in order to crush the enemies of Thy Church and to restore Divine Worship, didst vouchsafe to elect blessed Pius to the Supreme Pontificate, grant us to be defended by his patronage and so to cleave unto Thy service that, overcoming all the snares of the enemy, we may rejoice in perpetual peace), and it was with filial love, with the confidence of one who knows his request will be granted, that he added the prayer from his seminary days: "*Concede, misericors Deus, fragilitati nostrae praesidium...*" (Grant, O merciful God, in defence of our frailty...).

His devotion as he said Mass edified the congregation. In the complete stillness, one could hear even his whispered words, spoken in the "secret" of the Canon, and it was thus that the missionary, who was standing alongside to assist him, learned the identity of the "Roman priest" who had thus simply replied to his question.

He learnt it through a variation of the Canon which he had never heard before, and had certainly never thought to hear in that remote corner of the universe: "*...una cum me indigno famulo tuo, quem gregi tuo praesse voluisti*" (...together with me, Thy unworthy servant, whom Thou hast willed to watch over Thy flock): the variation made for one sole, exceptional case: *Summus autem Pontifex cum celebrat dicit...* (The Supreme Pontiff when he celebrates says...). Controlling his astonishment, he continued to stand beside him and assist him until the end of Mass. Not a rubric was omitted, right down to the last one: "*Cum dicit 'Et Verbum caro factum est', genuflectit...*" (When he says 'And the Word was made flesh' he genuflects). When it was over, and the missionary had recited with him the *Canticum Trium Puerorum* in thanksgiving, he knelt before him and with bent head said:

"*Loquere, Domine: quis es tu?*" (Speak, Sir: who art thou?).

And he replied:

"*Utique, frater: ego sum Paulus...*" (Yes, my brother: I am Paul...).

He felt now that his life was at its end, and he asked of God only that he be granted what was necessary for him to carry out *what he had been told to do.*

The reparation which he had to make personally he had effected before that handful of people in his last, first Mass on a lonely Tibetan mountain-top. Now he had to make a reparation valid for all men before the world, *ex Cathedra;* and his *cathedra* was the poor chair on which they had gently set him down. It was from here that he issued his last Decree, which the Vatican newspaper published with an extensive Italian summary of which we give a following translation.

PAULUS EPISCOPUS

SERVUS SERVORUM DEI

AD PERPETUAM REI MEMORIAM

Venerabiles Frates et dilecti Filii, salutem et Apostolicam Benedictionem.

Dei, profecto, imperscrutabili consilio atque infinitae misericordiae visum est (Eius, nimirum, qui *percutiendo sanat et ignoscendo conservat;* tum etiam, *culpa offenditur, poenitentia placatur*) graviter Nos, et fere mortifere, vulnerare corpore ut sanaret animo, ad eum finem, dumtaxat, ut *poenitentia aliquando conversi, Fratres Nostros, tandem, in fide confirmaremus.*

Dicent, autem, ii ad quos Supremae hoc Potestatis Nostrae Apostolicae documentum fuit commissum ut rite sollemniterque illud publici iuris facerent promulgarentque, quonam modo potens illa Dei manus Nos in ipso itinere sit consequuta et corripuerit, Roma abeuntem, ut deinde (sicut ultro libenterque Ipsi fatemur) Romam, translato sensu, denuo tandem reportaret, suam Ipsius sanctorumque Apostolorum Petri et Pauli indignationem contra Nos partam (ea potissimum de causa, quod loco decesserimus atque etiam quod, ob Nostram infirmitatem fragilitatemque animi, lege *orandi* atque, *idcirco, credendi,* tum denique *operandi,* Ecclesiam quoque Sanctam Catholicam inde abire passi fuerimus), ultimo, Nobis, in benedictionem verteret.

163

Haec volumus significare de iis omnibus, ut aiunt, "innovationibus" quae sub nomine "reformationum liturgicarum" (spiritu, vero, quodam pravo, Romanae Ecclesiae penitus infesto), continuo, post actum perfectumque Concilium Vaticanum II, divinum illum perantiquuumque Cultum Sacrorum Rituum Romanae Ecclesiae ejusdem adeo detorserunt atque in pessimam sane partem depravaverunt, ut illum quis jam amplius nequeat agnoscere: id aegre ferentibus et mirantibus omnibus, consternatisque, potissimum, quam maxime, ubique locorum Christi fidelibus.

Jam enim factum est, ut, ea de causa, iter miserrime stratum atque patefactum fuerit, innumerabilibus quibusque erroribus, sive in ordine dogmaticarum veritatum, sive religionis profitendae, sive morum sanctitatis tuendae: tum etiam ingentibus, omne genus, excessibus, licentiis, intemperantiis, insaniis, et prorsus hucusque inultis libidinum inventis, effrenationibus intolerabilibusque abominationibus quibus vel ipsa Templa maxima, et innumerae Domus Dei per orbem dispersae (*Domus*, inquimus, *orationis,* quae, testibus Nobis ipsis, semper sacra et inviolata loca extiterunt) turpiter inquinatae, saepe saepius, profanationibus, inventae sunt, auctoribus vel ipsis, non semel (quod enixe est lugendum, deprecandum, omni vi damnandum, tum vero indignissime omnino ferendum) sacris non paucis administris Ecclesiae Sanctae Catholicae.

Insanus, equidem, hic impetus furensque rabies, pessimorum quorumcumque *iconoclastarum propria,* a Nobis jam denuntiata confestim et reprobata (quam, tamen, strenue reprimere, eheu, minime contendimus), omnia prorsus reformandi, radicitus autem ea evertendo atque diruendo: amens quoque, potissimum, illud bellum exortum contra id omne quod "romanum" saperet in Liturgiae Ritibus, inito prius, nimirum, proelio acerrimo adversus Latinam linguam (quae est *Ecclesiae propria*), summum, tandem, calamitatis culmen obtigit, et in voraginem profundam nimis, detrusit omnia infaustissima dies illa qua Nos ipsi, vehementissime, licet, inviti atque ingenti quadam "vi prava" adstricti et veluti obruti (nimia favente, etiam, lugenda illa Nostra infirmitate animi), Constitutione Apostolica, data Ecclesiae, tertio Nonas Apriles, anni MCMLXIX, perantiquum illud, et venerabile Missale Romanum, cum alio, Novi Ordinis, Missali... miserrime, tandem, permutari concessimus.

Illud quoque, confestim factum est, ut, raptim, nec opinate, idem "Missale Novum" (Nobis sane, iterum iterumque invitis, secreto corde Nostro) valere inciperet pridie Kalendas Decembres ejusdem anni.

Omnes, continuo, et impensissime, noverunt (et ipsi sunt, non semel, experti quam celeriter!) cujus detrimenti, eversionis, naufragii, exitii atque ingentissimae ruinae pro unitate, concordia, fide, pietate catholicorum omnium, necnon pro ceterorum christiani nominis virorum non catholicorum conversione, illud Nostrum gravissimum Documentum causa maxima extiterit.

Quod ad Nos attinet, humillime profitemur, hodie solummodo, castigationis magnae verberibus merito percussos, quam Nobis immensa intulit misericordia Dei; in Ejus autem venia enixe sperantes, germano quoque Nostro accedente proposito animi, congruae, quamprimum, malorum reparationis instaurandae; dulcissimae, insuper, confisos Dei Genitricis, matris quoque Nostrae, Mariae Virginis, necnon Beatorum Apostolorum Petri et Pauli, Sancti etiam Praedecessoris Nostri Pii papae V cunctorumque intercessione, pacem illam, tandem, aliquando Nos repetisse, quam eadem ipsa misericordia Dei corde Nostro abstulerat, nec, ut par est, Nobis hucusque restituerat.

Quapropter, sine mora, a simplici intentione ad actus progredientes, his Litteris, Nostra manu signatis et *motu vere proprio* confectis, volumus ut sit inrita et ut ab omnibus prorsus abrogata habeatur Nostra illa Constitutio Apostolica *Missale Romanum* (quae, ceterum, nihil aliud habet Nostrum quam subscriptionem), qua Novus Ordo Missae fuit iniunctus.

Insuper, inritos omnino esse declaramus ceteros quoque Actus, sive anteriores, sive posteriores, qui eidem pertineant, aut quemlibet, cum ea, respectum habeant.

Huic abrogationi necessario sequitur velle Nos omnino, ex hoc nunc, Missale Romanum veteris Ordinis in pristinum plenissimumque vigorem restituere: de plenitudine, autem, Apostolicae potestatis Nostrae edicimus, ut idem illud Missale perantiquum exinde et in perpetuum ab omnibus usurpetur, in virtute sanctae oboedientiae, ut textus unicus, ad licite celebrandum sacrosanctum Missae Sacrificium, sicut praeteritis gloriosissimis temporibus (quatuor, nempe, ininterruptorum saeculorum decursu) adusque initum Concilium Vaticanum II, continenter, et sine controversia ulla, factum est.

Unicum illud esse volumus Missale, inquimus (ut iisdem, nimirum, fere verbis utamur, quibus Ecclesia illud promulgabat, "perpetuo valitura Constitutione"), "nempe ut Sacerdotes quibus precibus uti... quos Ritus... quasve Caeremonias in Missarum celebratione retinere, posthac, debeant".

Eadem suprema auctoritate Nostra abrogamus, insuper, omnes illas "innovationes", quae stultissime fuerunt immissae, in maximi quoque momenti Libris catholici Cultus: nempe in Rituali, in Pontificali, in Breviario, in Kalendario Sanctorum: praeterea, quod ad sacros Cantus attinet, in Libro Usuali musices Gregorianae illius, quae nullo prorsus praetextu est amittenda, poshabenda, aut cum recentibus neniis (sive vernacula lingua cantilenis, cithararum, minus minusve, instrumentis comitantibus) fas erit, exinde in posterum, permutari.

Maxima autem sollicitudine permoti, pro Sanctae totius Ecclesiae Catholicae unitate comparanda, strenueque in aevum tuenda, PRAECIPIMUS, in virtute sanctae oboedientiae, ut Lingua Latina, quam suavis recordationis antecessor Noster Joannes papa XXIII monuit esse "mirabile unitatis signum atque veritatis christianae integre tuendae instrumentum", ab omnibus sacris administris sedulo resumatur, atque, ut est re vera, "Lingua Ecclesiae viva" religiosa veneratione colatur et usurpetur.

In altum, idcirco, rursus erigatur, ut ubique circum, longe lateque luceat praefulgens "Cereus" ille, *cujus nimis lugenda extinctio* (ut Ipsi jamdiu praesensimus, et apertis verbis monuimus), *toti Ecclesiae Dei aegritudinem ac moestitiam fuisset latura.*

Noverint ergo cuncti, omni asseveratione velle Nos affirmare, et omnino ratos, nunc etiam temporis, iterum plene valere, Actus illos Supremi Magisterii Apostolici, qui, utcumque, respiciunt praefata argumenta huius Nostrae Litterae; videlicet: Encyclica *Mediator Dei*, Pii papae XII, deinde Constitutionem Apostolicam *Veterum Sapientia*, Joannis papae XXIII, tum denique Nostram Litteram Apostolicam *Sacrificium Laudis.*

167

Faxit misericors Deus, ut, perinde ac, hucusque, in mentis perturbatione et errore lugendissimo Fratres et Filii Nostri secuti sunt, iidem Nos quoque sequantur poenitentes, in via salutis, iterum reperta feliciter.

Illis, autem, optamus adjumento sit, sicut Nobis oratio eorum apud Deum, ita illis suavissima haec Nostra, quam toto cordis affectu impertimur, Apostolica Benedictio.

Datum, e montibus Tibetanis, pridie Idus Julias...

PAULUS Papa VI

PAUL BISHOP

SERVANT OF THE SERVANTS OF GOD

FOR EVERLASTING MEMORY

Venerable Brothers and Beloved Sons, Greetings and Apostolic Benediction.

It has pleased the infinite mercy of Him Who "heals through His chastisement and preserves through His forgiveness", Who though "offended by our fault is appeased by our repentance" to chastise Us mortally in Our body that so He might heal Us in Our soul to the end that "converted and repentant We might confirm Our brethren in the Faith".

Those to whom this decree of Ours is entrusted for its publication and promulgation in due and proper form will tell how the mighty hand of God reached and smote Us as We journeyed far from Rome so that — as We now recognise — We might figuratively speaking be once more led back to Rome, thus transforming into blessing that indignation of His, and of His Holy Apostles Peter and Paul, for Our having strayed far from it and for having in Our weakness allowed the Church to stray from it both in her law of worship and consequently also in her law of faith and practice.

We refer to all those "innovations" which, after the Second Vatican Council, under the guise of "liturgical reforms", deformed Catholic worship in a pernicious

169

anti-Roman spirit, rendering it unrecognisable as such, to the amazement of everyone and the deep consternation of the faithful, and thus opening the way to innumerable dogmatic, religious and moral aberrations, as well as to incredible abuses of every kind and in every sector, especially on the part of the clergy, of which the nefarious manifestations are plainly to be seen by all.

This onslaught, or as it was once described, — though unhappily not suppressed — by Us, this "iconoclastic fury" for reforming everything through destruction, this wanton war against all that was Roman in the liturgy, began with the attack upon Latin, "the Church's own language", and reached its apex, or rather its lowest depth, in that abolition of the Roman Missal which, wrung from Us in Our weakness and in spite of Our reluctance, was decreed in the Apostolic Constitution *Missale Romanum* of April 3rd 1969, and given effect on the following 30th of November.

Everyone is well aware of what ruin this decree has wrought on the unity, concord, faith and devotion of Catholics as well as upon the conversions to Holy Mother Church of our non-Catholic brethren, already perplexed and discouraged by precedents of a similar nature. For Ourselves, under the lash of chastisement which the immense goodness of God has inflicted upon Us, in Our hope for pardon, in Our desire to make reparation, through the intercession of our sweet, beloved Mother Mary, of the blessed Apostles Peter and Paul, of Our saintly predecessor Pius V, and of all the Saints, we do declare that only today have we found again that peace which God's same goodness took from Our hearts and withheld from Us until this hour.

Passing, therefore, from intention to deed, we hereby abrogate in every respect that Apostolic Constitu-

170

tion *Missale Romanum,* in which there is nothing of Ours beyond the signature, and all other decrees, previous or subsequent, therewith connected: We thus restore to the Roman Missal its full validity, desiring that as in the past (a most glorious and uninterrupted past of four long centuries), it be from today and for the future the only text approved and valid for celebration of the Holy Mass: "wherefore let it be known to all priests" (to repeat the words with which the Church effected its promulgation by means of an unreformable Constitution) "what prayers, what rites, and what ceremonies they must use henceforth and forever in the celebration of Mass".

In the same way we hereby annul all those innovations rashly introduced into the fundamental texts of the Church's worship — the Liber Pontificalis, the Ritual, the Breviary, and the Calendar of the Saints — whilst we re-instate Gregorian Chant as the music of the Church, never again to be suppressed or replaced. Furthermore, solicitous as We are for the Church's unity, We prescribe that Latin, that wondrous "sign of unity and instrument guarding the integrity of Christian truth" — as said by Our immediate predecessor John XXIII — once more become what it always was, "the Church's own language", and that there thus be re-lit to shine out again in the Church the "candle" whose extinction, as we Ourselves had foreseen, was to bring "squalor and gloom to the entire Church of God". We therefore confirm all decrees of the Magisterium relating to this, and in especial manner, among those most recent, Pius XII's Encyclical *Mediator Dei,* John XXIII's Apostolic Constitution *Veterum Sapientia,* and Our own Apostolic Letter *Sacrificium Laudis.*

May God grant that, as they did in Our straying, so all of Our Brothers and Sons may follow Us henceforward on the true path we have found again; and as we hope for help through their prayers, so too may they derive benefit from Our Apostolic Benediction.

Given on the mountains of Tibet, July 13th...

Pope Paul VI

The Pope Lives On

He hastened to sign, as he felt his strength ebbing away, but once he had made his signature, it appeared to return. He was thus able to garner with his own hands the first fruits of the Church's return to her true self, after the long barren period which had accompanied the Reform. Converted by that Mass, the girl from the plane asked to be baptised, and he it was who made her a Christian and a Catholic, giving her the name of Paula, as she had asked. That over, he felt a great peace descend upon him both by reason of this and of the sign from heaven which had told him *what he had to do*. Stretching out his arms, then, he prayed: "*Nunc dimittis...*" (Now dost Thou dismiss...), and the Lord heard the prayer of His servant.

He had asked to be left there, where he had "refound himself", and there he remained; but he was not long alone. The missionaries and their flock were discovered, caught up with at last by the forces of Maoist atheism. With them still was the neophyte, the hostess who had in turn begun to preach the faith to her ex-fellow Buddhists. All of them were slain; and their graves formed a garland around him.

The ground where they lay, quickened by the blood of martyrs, was bright with grass and flowers when in Rome, from the balcony of the great Basilica, a voice proclaimed to the waiting world: *"Habemus Papam..."* (We have a Pope...) and great and universal was the joy it gave.

We have a Pope: and this, the certainty that the Pope was not dead but lived on, that despite the tumult of the waves, the ship which carried Peter's emblem still rode sound and safe for all, this did indeed gladden the hearts of all who, whether followers or not of that emblem, men of little faith or none, had feared that the only hope of survival for all might perish in the storm.

That the Dream Come True

A dream, Your Holiness, just a bad dream: in which the only bit of beauty, the only happy and deep-felt consideration lies in the implicit wish that You may *see as many years as those allotted to Peter*, still continuing to serve the Church, *not shunning the burden*, no matter how heavy the Keys and how humanly justifiable the desire to lay them down before your *tempus resolutionis* (hour of dissolution) is at hand.

I was completing these pages yesterday as Your aeroplane landed in Rome. It was restoring You to us after a longer and more fatiguing journey than the present imaginary one, a journey which — *in itineribus semper* (in journeyings always), like the Apostle, and like him also *stoned*, but not just once — had even exposed You in Manila to the peril of assassins, his *periculis latronum* — and You came down the steps with such freshness and vigour as to convince us that Your hour of dissolution, according to human calculations, is still far from being at hand, and Your last journey, that with which You will *finish the race*, a long way off.

And so, perturbed as we are by certain reports which claim to interpret Your intentions, we would say to You as Martin's disciples did to him: "*Cur nos, Pater, deseris? aut cui nos desolatos relinquis? Invadent enim gregem tuum lupi rapaces*" (Why, Father, do You abandon us? or to whom will You leave us in

175

our desolation? Rapacious wolves will descend upon Your flock).

Wolves! The wolves, alas, have not still to fall upon Your flock: they are doing so, have already done so. Openly or disguised in their sheeps' clothing, they are already slaughtering it. Your task it is to fend them off. You it is who, barring the gate, the *ostium* that was opened in Your name by men of ill-faith to these "robbers and brigands", must now defend and save us. Yours is the task, and since God in His mercy has given You the time and the means to carry it out, You cannot, must not leave it to others. You cannot let pass to others the task and the merit of giving back the Church to herself by restoring her oneness in truth, by rendering to her that "Bond of Union" which is her language, her music, and her rites, *by giving her back, with all that this signifies, her Holy Mass.*

Her Holy Mass! No one ever expressed and proved more logically or feelingly the fact that the Mass should never have been touched than did You Yourself in the Allocution, almost a plea, which You pronounced just a year ago. Your said then it had seemed *destined* to enjoy an untouchable immutability... *Destined* to give us the comfort of loyalty to a spiritual past which we in turn would continue and pass on to the generations to come; You spoke of its "angelic tongue", and its "stupendous, incomparable music" And yet, (in spite of You, despite Your reluctance — but will that avail You *in die illa?*) it was not only touched, but manhandled, and then finally it was eliminated with a contempt which finds precedent and equivalent only in that shown by Luther for the Popish Mass that had to be destroyed because upon it "as upon a rock, rests the Papacy", which is to say, the Church.

To You, then — and to whom else should we or can we go if not to You — do we address our sorrowful supplication: for the love that we bear You, for the love that You bear the Church, restore to her — let us say it with the poet — "the voice of prayer", of her own prayer: *give the Church back her Mass!*

It is the lowliest of those millions of Your devoted children, and therefore the most acceptable to Your own humilty, who begs and beseeches this of You on bended knees in the name of all the others. Their cry of grief does not reach Your ears; by that sad privilege of the great who must only know what pleases, only hear the voice of praise, it is not permitted to reach You.

Give us back our Mass: The Mass "of our forebears and that of our Saints", as You called it in Your Allocution. It is also the Mass of our Martyrs. It was for this, for their "loyalty to the Roman Mass" that the Forty Martyrs whom You have but lately canonised glady laid down their lives.

Give us back our Mass, and so put an end to other martyrdoms — the white martyrdoms of desire — perhaps unknown to You, but not to one who, having espoused this cause, has become confidant to so much human suffering: the martyrdoms of all those priests who pray God not to see that "Advent of 1971" which is intended to put an end for them all to that Mass for which *their hands were, and remain, consecrated.*

We say intended to, for we still wish to believe that it cannot happen: that if You are prevented from imitating Paschal II and saying like him "What I did, I did as a man and do condemn it", You will at least, in that magnanimity which is characteristic of truth, follow the example of your other predecessor — the Saint with whom and against whom You have been so foolishly placed in contrast — and grant to all *in perpetuo* the "dispensation" or faculty to celebrate the *unchanging* Mass, with its language, rites, and plainsong to enshrine its unchanging *Credo*, the *Credo* of Your own *Professio Fidei* which is, again, the expression of its *Adoro*.

We are aware, Holy Father, that this will be hard for You: that many obstacles will be raised against the enactment of Your will, and not least of them, possibly first of them, that of money: the great amount of money that the Reform brings to large numbers of people — (the new texts, no longer in the sacred common language, all have their Copyright clearly displayed in the common language of commerce): that money which possesses no ill-odour (*pecunia non olet*) — not even for those noble champions of the "Church of the Poor": the money which everything obeys (*pecuniae oboediunt omnia*), yes, even the professional protestors of every manner of alleged protest. — But still harder would it be for You *contra stimulum calcitrare* (to kick against the goad) — and you will say to those vested interests what Peter said to the man of Samaria: *Pecunia tua tecum sit!* (Let money be your portion!). For we know that You are jealous, and it could not be otherwise, for one interest alone, the supreme and only interest which is that of God.

Give us back, then, at least our Mass — as much for Your sake, if one may say so, as for ours. Your name cannot be linked through future centuries to a monstruous, unthinkable, incredible piece of absurdity whereby from a "pluralism", a liturgical "pantheism"

178

which finds room for all gods, not excluding Priapus, and for all rites however and by whomsoever conjured up, only one would be excluded: only one Mass would be outlawed — that "of our forebears and that of our Saints", the one which was made to last as long as the world ("*perpetuo valitura*") and from the world to bring us to the Mass which is eternal.

Should this not take place, if *even this* dispensation, this unlimited *vacatio* were to be denied, then we should be afflicted by the greatest yet of all our misfortunes. We could no longer love the Pope. No longer could we feel ourselves to be his loving children, but only his subjects: subjects cold and resigned; — (for nothing, let us be clear, no motive, no bitterness, no pain — could ever separate us from the Church). — And we should begin again to say the same prayer for You now that we said for You in June seven years ago when You were about to be elected: the prayer begging God to give us, to restore to us, in You "*Pontificem illum qui et pio in nos studio semper tibi placitus e tuo populo pro salubri regimine sit assidue ad gloriam tui nominis reverendus...*" (A Pope who will be ever pleasing to Thee in his highest care for us and who will be deeply revered by Thy people for conducting all things well to the glory of Thy name).

That this may come about, we repeat, with all the insistence of children towards a father, that we want You to remain with us. We want You to say, like Martin, to Him who gave You the Keys: "*Domine, si adhuc populo tuo sum necessarius, non recuso laborem...*" (Lord, if still I am necessary for Thy people, I shall not shun the task), and on that day it will indeed seem to us that we have been dreaming.

Holy Father, grant us our petition: make the beauty of our dream quickly come true; and let the hand, which once was raised in paternal severity to admonish this Your loving son, now be raised again over him, but this time to bless and console. Any excess of which he may seem guilty comes solely from excess of love.

NOTES

[1] Encyclical *Veterum Sapientia*. - [2] *Osservatore Romano* 8-9 March 1965. - [3] Newspapers and magazines spoke of it in April 1970 on the occasion of the death of the Patriarch Alexis. - [4] *Le Figaro* 18 December 1969. - [5] GIOVANNI SCANTAMBURLO, *Perchè il Concilio non ha condannato il Comunismo*. - [6] Letter to the Cardinal Secretary of State, *Osservatore Romano*, 4 February 1970. - [7] *La Croix*, 30 March 1970. - [8] *Osservatore Romano*, 12 June 1969. - [9] Quoted by FELIX LACAMBRE, 11 June 1969. - [10] Quoted by Reverend CARLO BOYER, *Osservatore Romano*, 26-27 October 1970. - [11] *Die Presse*, 11 June 1969. - [12] 12 June 1969. - [13] *Una Voce*, Paris, March-April 1970. - [14] Quoted in my book *Super Flumina Babylonis*. - [15] *Osservatore Romano*, 14 August 1969. - [16] Encyclical *Mediator Dei*. - [17] *Osservatore Romano*, 23 April 1970. - [18] Apostolic Letter *Sacrificium Laudis*. - [19] *Acta Apostolicae Sedis*, 9 September 1968. - [20] Rome Vicariate, 29 November 1968. - [21] VIRGILIO NOÈ, *Osservatore Romano*, 29 May 1970. - [22] *Osservatore Romano*, 5 February 1970. - [23] *Relazioni*, June 1970. - [24] Cardinal SIRI, *In the General Assembly of the Italian Bishops*, April 1970. - [25] *Osservatore Romano*, 30 June - 1 July 1970. - [26] *Osservatore Romano*, 30 June - 1 July 1970. - [27] Audience to the Lombard Seminary in Rome, *Osservatore Romano*, 8 December 1968. - [28] *Osservatore Romano*, 12 November 1970. - [29] Audience with the Bishops of the Permanent Secretariate of the Synod, 15 May 1970. - [30] LOUIS BOUYER, *La Décomposition du Catholicisme*, and See ALFREDO CATTABIANI, *Osservatore Romano*, 30 January 1969. - [31] Encyclical *Mysterium Fidei*. - [32] Letter written by Cardinal LERCARO on the Liturgical Reform, 1965. - [33] *Osservatore Romano*, 21 February 1968. - [34] From the Allocution quoted in my book *Super Flumina Babylonis*. - [35] *Osservatore Romano*, 19 April 1969. - [36] RAYMOND DULAC, *La Messe de Saint-Pierre-aux-liens*, in *Itineraires*, February 1970. - [37] JEAN MADIRAN, *Le processus de la communion dans la main*, in *Itineraires*, July -August 1969. - [38] Monsignor NESTOR ADAM, Bishop of Sion, *Osservatore Romano*, 11 January 1970. - [39] *Osservatore Romano*, 4 September 1970. - [40] 19 October 1967. - [41] Quoted by *La Courte-reforme Catholique*, February 1970. - [42] *Formula Missae*, quoted by *Le Courrier de Rome*, No. 51. - [43] *Contra Henricum Regem Angliae* and *Sermo Dominicae I Adventus*. - [44] *Osservatore Romano*, 27 November 1969. - [45] Monsignor DOMENICO CELADA, *Realtà Politica*, 15 November 1969. - [46] *Figaro Litteraire*, 14-20 October 1968. - [47] Quoted by PIERRE TILLOY, *L'Unité dans l'heresie*. - [48] *Osservatore Romano*, 6 November 1969. - [49] CARLO BELLI,

Il Tempo, 30 November 1969. - [50] VIRGILIO LEVI, *Osservatore Romano*, 1 December 1969. - [51] *Osservatore Romano*, 31 October 1969. - [52] *Osservatore Romano*, 13 May 1970. - [53] *Saint Vincent de Paul... Entretiens*, tome XII. - [54] FABRIZIO DE SANTIS, *Le Dodici Tavole dei "Progressisti"*, from Brussels to *Corriere della Sera*, 18 September 1970. - [55] EMILIO CAVATERRA, *Amore in convento e sport in chiesa*, in *Giornale d'Italia*, 20-21 November 1970. - [56] *Il Giornale d'Italia*, 17 September 1970. - [57] LORENZO BEDESCHI, *Il Cardinale Destituito*. - [58] *Saggio sulla Religione*. - [59] 4 October 1970.

www.ingramcontent.com/pod-product-compliance
Lightning Source LLC
Chambersburg PA
CBHW021505090426

42739CB00007B/467